"This concise and vigorous bc
joy to read. Each hard-hitting
the biblical text, references R ... wisdom, and points to God in Christ. This energetic manifesto will be of value for personal study, small-group discussion, and classroom reading at a beginning-college level."

Robert W. Yarbrough, Professor of New Testament,
Covenant Theological Seminary

"I am thrilled that Tim Chester has addressed this neglected fruit of the Spirit. When the Reformation happened, it was, among other things, a rediscovery of true Christian joy. This joy had suffused the Christian world of the New Testament but throughout the medieval era had been largely forgotten as being central to the Christian life. Thus it is no wonder that when, in the eighteenth century, the Reformed author Andrew Fuller was seeking a revival among his fellow Baptists in England, he asked the ever-pertinent query, 'Why is it that Christians in the present day come so far short of the primitive Christians in the possession of joy?' He knew, as did the Reformers, and Paul before them all, that whenever a renewal or revival of the Christian faith takes place, joy will abound!"

Michael A. G. Haykin, Professor of Church History and
Biblical Spirituality, The Southern Baptist Theological Seminary;
Director, Andrew Fuller Center for Baptist Studies

"Charles Spurgeon once told his congregation, 'It is a great privilege to meet a truly happy man, a graciously happy man.' Let it never be said that *Reformed* and *joy* are uneasy cohabitants in the heart of a Christian. Tim Chester's work is a much-needed reminder for Reformed Christians that because we have been saved by grace alone, we of all people have reason to live out our days with deep exuberance over such a great salvation. In this volume, you will meet some truly happy men from the past—happy because they recovered a glorious gospel and happy because, in so doing, they restored to the church deep and lasting joy in Jesus. Read, remember, and rejoice! People of grace should be a graciously happy people."

Jeff Robinson Sr., Senior Editor, The Gospel Coalition;
Pastor-Teacher, Christ Fellowship Church, Louisville, Kentucky

"Tim Chester has a well-earned reputation as a writer of clear, accessible, and helpful books for Christians. This is no exception. In a remarkably short space, he moves repeatedly from Luther to Galatia to Paul and to the present day, offering an account of numerous facets of the gospel, a plea for the Reformation understanding of faith and justification, and a vision of what the church is. And at every step of the way, he presses home the importance of joy as part of the content and the goal of the Christian life—though not joy as the world understands it but that which comes from knowing and resting on Christ. A great read!"

Carl R. Trueman, Professor of Biblical and Religious Studies, Grove City College

"We live in a world that tells us to look within ourselves to find joy and lasting happiness. The problem is, looking within leaves us empty-handed, hopeless under the weight of our own unrighteousness. But Tim Chester has a message of remarkable hope. True joy is found in Christ and Christ alone. With help from the apostle Paul and the Protestant Reformers, Chester challenges the church today to return to the Scriptures, for they are the swaddling cloths of Christ. There we will hear the call from Christ himself to put aside our worthless merit and trust in him alone for a righteousness he alone can provide. Only then will we rediscover joy that will not disappoint."

Matthew Barrett, Associate Professor of Christian Theology, Midwestern Baptist Theological Seminary; editor, The Five Solas Series

"Tim Chester brings the core truths of the Reformation—'by grace alone, through faith alone, in Christ alone'—to life. This is not a dry tour of history but rather an invitation to rediscover the joy that Paul unpacks in Galatians and that brought Luther to lead a gospel revolution 1,500 years later. If *joy* is not the first word that comes to your mind when you think about the Reformation, you need to read this book! You could read it in a day, but its impact will last long beyond that."

Jeremy McQuoid, Teaching Pastor, Deeside Christian Fellowship Church, Aberdeen, Scotland

Reforming Joy

Other Crossway Books by Tim Chester

Everyday Church: Gospel Communities on Mission (coauthored with Steve Timmis)

Good News to the Poor: Social Involvement and the Gospel

A Meal with Jesus: Discovering Grace, Community, and Mission around the Table

Total Church: A Radical Reshaping around Gospel and Community (coauthored with Steve Timmis)

Why the Reformation Still Matters (coauthored with Michael Reeves)

You Can Change: God's Transforming Power for Our Sinful Behavior and Negative Emotions

Reforming Joy

A Conversation between Paul, the Reformers, and the Church Today

Tim Chester

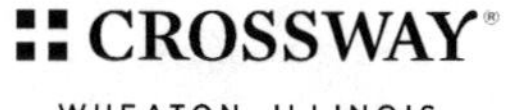

WHEATON, ILLINOIS

Reforming Joy: A Conversation between Paul, the Reformers, and the Church Today

Published by Crossway
1300 Crescent Street
Wheaton, Illinois 60187

Originally published as *Rediscovering Joy: The Dynamic Power of the Reformation in Galatians* by Inter-Varsity Press, London, England, 2017. North American edition published in 2018 by permission of Inter-Varsity Press.

Cover design: Peter Voth

First North American printing 2018

Printed in the United States of America

All emphases in Scripture quotations have been added by the author.

Trade paperback ISBN: 978-1-4335-5842-9
ePub ISBN: 978-1-4335-5845-0
PDF ISBN: 978-1-4335-5843-6
Mobipocket ISBN: 978-1-4335-5844-3

Library of Congress Cataloging-in-Publication Data

Names: Chester, Tim, author.
Title: Reforming joy : a conversation between Paul, the reformers, and the church today / Tim Chester.
Other titles: Rediscovering joy
Description: Wheaton : Crossway, 2018. | "Originally published as Rediscovering Joy: The Dynamic Power of the Reformation in Galatians by Inter-Varsity Press, London, England, 2017." | Includes bibliographical references and index. |
Identifiers: LCCN 2017052809 (print) | LCCN 2018025545 (ebook) | ISBN 9781433558436 (pdf) | ISBN 9781433558443 (mobi) | ISBN 9781433558450 (epub) | ISBN 9781433558429 (tp)
Subjects: LCSH: Bible. Galatians—Criticism, interpretation, etc. | Bible. Galatians—Textbooks. | Joy—Biblical teaching. | Reformation.
Classification: LCC BS2685.52 (ebook) | LCC BS2685.52 .C44 2018 (print) | DDC 227/.40609—dc23
LC record available at https://lccn.loc.gov/2017052809

Crossway is a publishing ministry of Good News Publishers.

VP 27 26 25 24 23 22 21 20 19 18
15 14 13 12 11 10 9 8 7 6 5 4 3 2 1

CONTENTS

Introduction

LET'S TALK ABOUT JOY

This book is a three-way conversation. We'll start in sixteenth-century Europe with the Reformation. We'll travel back to first-century Galatia and the foundations of the Reformation in the message of Paul. And then we'll come home and explore their relevance in the twenty-first century.

It's going to be a conversation about joy.

Suppose someone asked you what it feels like being a Christian—not what you *do* or what you *believe* but what you *feel* as a Christian. Would you say, "It's a life of joy"? In Galatians 4:15, Paul asks, "Where is that joyful and grateful spirit you felt then?" (NLT). When Paul first knew the Galatians, they were full of joy. But now their joy has gone. Maybe when you first became a Christian, you were full of excitement. You couldn't quite believe your sins were forgiven; you were part of God's family; you had confidence for the future. But now your joy has gone. It all feels routine. Now you speak of duty, responsibility, obligation. You speak of getting on with it or knuckling down. All good stuff, but it's not animated by joy. So the Christian life feels like hard work. Or maybe you look with suspicion on those excitable Christians.

The cheesy smiles. The unremitting enthusiasm. The hearts on sleeves. You've grown cynical and detached.

This letter of Galatians was written to Christians who had lost their joy. False teachers had turned up saying something like this: "It's great that you've been saved by faith in Jesus. But the real mark of God's people is keeping God's law. That's what will keep you on track." It sounds very plausible. But the result is lost joy. Stolen joy. It's a message that "pretends to be the Good News," says Paul, "but is not the Good News at all" (Gal. 1:6–7, NLT). So Paul brings the Galatians back to two fountains of joy: faith in Christ and life in the Spirit.

It was these same issues that fueled the Reformation. The year 2017 marks the five hundredth anniversary of one of the key moments that launched the Reformation: the nailing of the "Ninety-Five Theses" to the door of the Castle Church in Wittenberg, Germany, by Martin Luther. The letter to the Galatians was one of the driving forces of Luther's rediscovery of gospel joy. In his early life he had been an Augustinian monk. In 1512, when he was twenty-nine years old, he was sent to teach at the new university at Wittenberg. So Luther began to lecture on the Psalms, Romans, and Galatians. It was through immersing himself in these books that he came to realize that the message of the medieval Catholic Church didn't match the message of the Bible. What he heard from the church brought condemnation. In contrast, what he heard from the Scriptures was good news. The Reformation was a rediscovery of joy.

I hope this conversation will give you a better understanding of the Reformation and its roots in the message of the New Testament. But above all, my prayer is that, together, we'll rediscover and be reformed by joy.

Think of this book as a time machine. Hop on board, and to start, we'll set the dial for October 31, 1517, in the town of Wittenberg . . .

1

HOW TO HEAR GOD'S VOICE

The Reforming Joy of Scripture Alone (Galatians 1)

No movement begins with a single moment. But October 31, 1517, has justifiably come to symbolize the start of the Reformation. This was the date on which Martin Luther nailed his "Ninety-Five Theses" to the door of the Castle Church in Wittenberg. This document would have competed with other pieces of paper, for the door served as a kind of public forum—like a modern urban wall covered in posters or a bulletin board on the village green. Luther was trying to instigate a public debate.

The "Ninety-Five Theses" was primarily a complaint about the abuse of indulgences. The medieval church taught that when most people died, they went to a temporary place of torment called *purgatory*, which "purged" you of sin before you graduated to heaven. Indulgences promised to reduce the time you or a loved one spent in purgatory. And the church sold these indulgences for cash. The local archbishop complained about Luther to the pope, and the pope threatened to excommunicate Luther. But this opposition simply made Luther more radical. He began to attack the authority of the pope. So in 1521, Emperor Charles V summoned Luther to defend himself with the promise of safe conduct.

At this time there were no denominations. In Western Europe there was just the one church of Rome. So on one side of the debate was this church with all its infrastructure, personnel, wealth, history, power, and tradition. It represented every parish church in Europe. On the other side was one man, Martin Luther—one man and his Bible. Luther told the emperor at this meeting that if anyone could refute his errors from the Scriptures, then he would be the first to throw his writings into the fire. The imperial advocate pushed the monk for an answer: Would he recant or not? Luther replied, "Unless I am convicted of error by the Scriptures, . . . and my conscience is taken captive by God's word, I cannot and will not recant anything, for to act against our conscience is neither safe for us nor open to us. On this I take my stand. I can do no other. God help me. Amen."[1]

The Most Wanted Man in Europe

Ten years later a messenger visited the house of Stephen Vaughan, the agent of King Henry VIII in Antwerp. The messenger offered to lead Vaughan to a "friend" who wanted to talk with him. Vaughan pressed him for a name but without success. Nevertheless, Vaughan followed him through the streets and out beyond the city walls. There in a field was the mysterious stranger. "Do you not know me?" he asked. "My name is Tyndale."

William Tyndale was the most wanted man in Europe. Back in London his translation of the New Testament was being publicly burned. People found with a copy were being tortured. But Tyndale had heard that the king was interested in negotiating a deal. At a second meeting Tyndale promised that, if the king would allow an English Bible, any English Bible—it didn't have to be Tyndale's translation—then he would stop writing and return to England. There the king could do with him as he liked. Tyndale was willing to trade torture and death for the publication of an English Bible. No such undertaking came, and Tyndale never returned home. Four years later he was betrayed by a spy and executed by order of Emperor Charles V.

At stake for both Luther and Tyndale was joy. When Tyndale first published an English New Testament in 1526, he included a reading guide. The New Testament, he said, is the gospel, and the gospel "signifies good, merry, glad and joyful tidings, that make a man's heart glad, and make him sing, dance, and leap for joy." He added,

> Now can the wretched man (that is wrapped in sin, and is in danger to death and hell) hear no more joyous a thing, than such glad and comfortable tidings of Christ. So he cannot but be glad and laugh from the low bottom of his heart, if he believe that the tidings are true.[2]

There is nothing "more joyous" than the "joyous tidings" in the Bible that make us "leap for joy." You get the picture: the Bible matters because it leads to joy. You might even laugh from "the low bottom of your heart."

The Reformation was the rediscovery of justification by faith alone in the work of Christ. But the *foundation* of the Reformation was the ultimate authority of Scripture alone. The majority of people, including the most powerful and most educated, said one thing. Scripture taught another. And the Reformers chose Scripture.

Tyndale wrote, "The scripture is the touchstone that trieth all doctrines, and by [which] we know the false from the true. . . . The scripture is a light, and sheweth us the true way, both what to do and what to hope for; and a defence from all error, and a comfort in adversity."[3] It is God's Word that "is the chiefest of the apostles, and pope, and Christ's vicar, and head of the Church, and head of the general council."[4] In other words, the authority of the Bible is greater than any human institution or individual.

If we reset the dial of our time machine to first-century Galatia, we'll discover that it wasn't a new struggle. Indeed, Paul's letter to the Galatians was one of the key texts that shaped the Reformation. Galatians 1:6–7 says, "I am astonished that you are so quickly deserting him who called you in the grace of Christ and are turning to a different gospel—not that there is another one."

What was at stake in Galatia and the Reformation was the gospel. The word "gospel" means "good news." The gospel is the good news that our sins are forgiven and that we've been rescued (1:4). It answers the question, How can we be right with God and escape his judgment?

But what happens when you have competing answers to that question—as was the case in Galatia, in the Reformation, and today? How do we know which is the true gospel? Where's the true source of joy?

We'll address this issue by asking a series of connected questions.

How Do We Know What's True?

In Galatia one answer to the question of how we know what's true was this: "You should submit to the founding church in

Jerusalem." People had come from Jerusalem telling the Gentiles (the non-Jews) that they needed to be circumcised. How do you know the true gospel? The Jerusalem church will tell you.

Jump in our time machine, head to the sixteenth century, and we find the Catholic Church effectively giving the same answer. The only difference is that because the apostle Peter moved to Rome, it's now the successor to Peter in Rome, the pope, who tells us what God wants.

Fast-forward to the twenty-first century, and we find a new variation on the answer. Today many people say, "I'll follow the one I like best." They say things like, "I'm not a Christian because I don't like the idea of a god who sends people to hell." That's about as logical as saying, "I don't believe in wearing a life jacket because I don't like the idea of drowning." Nevertheless, people think they can determine what's true on the basis of their preference, as if they construct reality through their decisions.

It's time to let the engine of the time machine cool down but not before we make the journey back to find Paul. He answers the question of how we can know what's true in Galatians 1:11–12: "For I would have you know, brothers, that the gospel that was preached by me is not man's gospel. For I did not receive it from any man, nor was I taught it, but I received it through a revelation of Jesus Christ."

Paul is contrasting human origins and divine revelation. On the one hand, we have knowledge based on human reason, human tradition, or human experience. All these things lead to some measure of truth. Just think of what human beings have discovered, invented, and created. But all these sources of knowledge have a limitation, and there's a clue in that word *human*. The problem is not reason, tradition, or experience; the problem is *human* reason, *human* tradition, and *human* experience. Human beings are made in the image of God, which means we're capable of amazing feats of discovery. But we're also fallen sinners, warped by our selfishness, determined not to obey God. And so our knowledge is always flawed. Our understanding is biased against God.

As a result, we need divine revelation. And we need it not just to top off our knowledge but also to realign our knowledge toward God. That's why Proverbs 1:7 says, "The fear of the LORD is the beginning of knowledge."

Here's the fundamental issue: When you have to choose, are you going to trust the creature or the Creator, the finite or the infinite, the lawbreaker or the lawmaker, the selfish offspring or the loving Father?

Where Do We Find Divine Revelation?

How do we know what's true? God has told us. But of course, that answer leads to another question: Where do we find this divine revelation?

The answer is in the testimony or preaching of the first apostles. Galatians 1:7–8 says, "There are some who trouble you and want to distort the gospel of Christ. But even if we or an angel from heaven should preach to you a gospel contrary to the one we preached to you, let him be accursed." And in case you missed the point, Paul says it a second time in 1:9: "As we have said before, so now I say again: If anyone is preaching to you a gospel contrary to the one you received, let him be accursed."

The true gospel is "the one we preached." The "we" here is "we apostles"—the people who had met the risen Christ and been appointed to testify about him. They could personally testify to what they had heard, seen, and touched (1 John 1:1–3).

In Galatians 1:1, Paul introduces himself by saying, "Paul, an apostle—not from men nor through man, but through Jesus Christ and God the Father, who raised him from the dead." It's important that Paul's readers (and that includes us) realize that Paul is God's messenger conveying God's message. His gospel is not something he or anyone else made up but a "revelation of Jesus Christ" (1:12).

We have this apostolic preaching or testimony in the New Testament. We can hold in our hands—amazingly—a message from God. God revealed himself in his Son, Jesus. That revelation in Jesus was promised through the Old Testament prophets and recorded by the New Testament apostles (2 Pet. 1:16–21). The Holy Spirit ensured that their testimony is accurate and true (John 14:26; 16:13). So the whole Bible is a message from God. It's where we hear God's voice.

So Paul says—and feel the strength in his words—"even if *we or an angel from heaven* should preach to you a gospel contrary to the one we preached to you, let him be accursed" (Gal. 1:8). Even apostles can't trump the apostolic preaching. The apostolic testimony is not the apostles' personal opinion. It's the Spirit-inspired record of God's revelation in Christ. In 2:11–13, we discover that when an apostle—in this case Peter—acted contrary to the apostolic gospel, he needed to be rebuked. Even apostles (and their papal successors, if you want to follow that line of argument) are subject to the Scriptures.

Indeed, Paul goes further. Imagine you read your Bible tonight before you go to bed. Then in the night you have a vision. And what a vision! An angel visits you and gives you a message from God. Paul says that in the morning you should obey your Bible. Our experience—however dramatic it feels at the time—never trumps Scripture (1:8).

Paul's words are a warning. He's astonished that the Galatians are deserting the true gospel (1:6). But don't miss the amazing good news. When you pick up your Bible, you hold in your hands a message from God. And it's a message more impressive, more intimate, and more reliable than a chat with any apostle or a vision of any angel!

Is the Bible Enough?

But who decides what the Scriptures say? That was the issue in the Reformation. The Catholic Church said that ordinary people weren't sophisticated enough to read the Bible. They would only misunderstand it. "We'll read the Bible for you," they said, "and tell you what to believe."

The Catholic Church eventually realized that it couldn't prevent an English translation of the Bible, so it produced its own version in 1582, the Rheims New Testament. Yet its preface still said,

> We must not imagine that in the primitive Church . . . the translated Bibles into the vulgar tongues, were in the hands of every husbandman [craftsman], prentice, boys, girls, mistress, maid, man. . . . No, in those better times men were neither so ill, nor so curious of themselves, so to abuse the blessed book of Christ.[5]

In other words, the church still disapproved of ordinary people reading the Bible! They feared them getting the wrong end of the stick and causing all sorts of trouble. In this view, authority is the Bible *plus* the tradition of the church.

It was the same issue in Galatia. The troublemakers weren't saying, "Follow us *instead* of following the Bible." They were saying, "You've misunderstood the Bible. Let us tell you what it really means. After all, we're from the founding church of Jerusalem."

Paul's response is to tell a lengthy two-part story. It's a fascinating response. His job would have been so much easier if he had just said, "Actually, the leaders of the church in Jerusalem agree with me." Because that was the case. In Galatians 2:3, Paul describes how in Jerusalem, "even Titus, who was with me, was not forced to be circumcised, though he was a Greek." In 2:9, he concludes, "When James and Cephas [Peter] and John, who seemed to be pillars, perceived the grace that was given to me, they gave the right hand of fellowship to Barnabas and me." Job done. Argument won.

But Paul doesn't go straight from 1:12 to 2:9. Instead, he gives a lengthy travel itinerary in 1:13–2:10. He describes how he received his message directly from Christ (1:13–16) and didn't even consult the apostles (1:16–24). If Paul had simply said, "The Jerusalem church agrees with me," then he would have won one battle at the expense of another. He would have won the one over circumcision, but he would have conceded that Gentile Christians needed to obey the Jerusalem church *rather than Scripture alone.*

Eventually, Paul did meet the leaders of the Jerusalem church, as he describes in chapter 2. Verse 2 says, "I went up . . . in order to make sure I was not running or had not run in vain." That might sound like he wants them to affirm his message. But that makes no sense of 2:5: "To them we did not yield in submission even for a moment, so that the truth of the gospel might be preserved for you." Paul won't compromise on the gospel. Too much is at stake. But neither does he want two churches to emerge—a Jewish church and a Gentile church. So in 2:2, he's not worried about whether they approve of *his message.* He's worried about whether they'll accept his *converts.* That's why he takes uncircumcised Titus as his test case. As it turns out, his fears are alleviated, and as we've just seen, Titus was not required to be circumcised (2:3).

But still Paul wants to make sure we know where true authority lies. So he picks his words carefully: "And from those who seemed to be influential (*what they were makes no difference to me; God shows no partiality*)—those, I say, who seemed influential added nothing to me" (2:6). Jerusalem is not God's favorite church, and it has no authority over Paul's ministry.

Paul isn't being churlish or uppity. He's determined that we should realize that authority comes from God's Word above all else. We're not called to obey God's Word plus a human institution or God's Word *interpreted* by a human institution—not even the founding church in Jerusalem.

So is the Bible enough? Yes. Our authority comes from Scripture alone.

What Does This Mean Today?

It's time to set our time machine for home. Few of us are under pressure to submit to a denomination or church body. Indeed, many of us would do well to trust ourselves less and trust the advice of older Christians more!

For us the challenge of *Scripture alone* comes primarily from the world around us:

- The world says human beings are essentially good. The Bible says we are sinners who face God's judgment.
- The world says it is arrogant to claim that Christianity is unique. The Bible says Jesus is the only way to God.
- The world says modern science has disproved many of the Bible's claims. The Bible claims to be the reliable Word of God.

- The world says human sexuality is a matter of personal preference. The Bible says sex is given within the context of marriage between a man and a woman.
- The world says gender is fluid. The Bible says gender is given to us at birth.
- The world says desire is sovereign. The Bible calls us to self-control and self-denial.
- The world says we are the victims of our circumstances. The Bible says our sinful desires shape how we respond to our circumstances.

Sometimes that pressure is full-on as Christians are attacked for their beliefs. But often it's more subtle, as our sense of what is "sensible" is reshaped by our culture. In 1 Corinthians 1:18, Paul says, "The word of the cross is folly to those who are perishing." The wisdom of the world *appears* wise, and the message of the cross *appears foolish*. When our society invites us to "reinterpret" the Bible in the light of scientific advances or accepted norms or psychological insights, it will *appear* wise. We will feel the pull away from the Scriptures.

But look at how Paul describes the work of Christ in Galatians 1:4: Christ "gave himself for our sins to deliver us from the present evil age." In our age people are saying that things we once thought of as wrong (like sex outside marriage) are in fact right and that things we once thought of as right (like self-denial and self-restraint) are in fact wrong. Our moral world is being turned upside down. But don't be deceived. This age is evil. It's going to pass into judgment. And Christ has rescued us from this passing age for a coming age—one that will be glorious and eternal.

What does this mean for us today? We must listen to God's Word above the voices of the world around us.

Am I Trying to Please People?

Our final question is more personal. It's one that we need to ask not of the Bible but of ourselves. Galatians 1:10 is key to understanding the issues in Galatia. Paul says, "For am I now seeking the approval of man, or of God? Or am I trying to please man? If I were still trying to please man, I would not be a servant of Christ."

Back in Galatia it was easy to portray Paul as a man pleaser. After all, he was the one saying that Gentiles didn't need to be circumcised. Think about that for a moment. Hearing that message in the days before anesthetic would certainly have pleased me!

But effectively what Paul is saying in 1:10 is this: "Consider my life as a servant of Christ. Think about the imprisonments, the mobs, and the beatings. If my priority were people's approval, I would have resigned as Christ's servant a long time ago!" In 6:17, he says, "I bear on my body the marks of Jesus." His opponents wanted the physical mark of circumcision to show a person's allegiance to Christ. "If you want physical marks," says Paul, "then let me lift up my shirt and show you the scars left by the fives times I was lashed, the three times I was beaten by rods, and the time I was stoned" (see 2 Cor. 11:24–25). These are the proof that Paul doesn't live to please people.

In fact, it's the circumcisers who are trying to win the approval of others. Galatians 6:12–13 says,

> It is those who want to make a good showing in the flesh who would force you to be circumcised, and only in order that they may not be persecuted for the cross of Christ. For even those who are circumcised do not themselves keep the law, but they desire to have you circumcised that they may boast in your flesh.

In other words, what's driving these people is not a commitment to the law—they themselves don't keep it, not the whole law of Moses. No, what's driving their demand for circumcision is a desire for the approval of their fellow Jews. They want the approval of their peers.

The challenge of *Scripture alone* is, Will we listen to God or to the world? But behind that is a bigger challenge: Do we live for God's or other people's approval? If the answer is other people's, then we'll inevitably end up compromising, neglecting, or reinterpreting the Bible to fit into the world around us. After all, no one wants to be thought of as a religious bigot or an outdated fool.

But Paul says, "Far be it from me to boast except in the cross of our Lord Jesus Christ, by which the world has been crucified to me, and I to the world" (6:14). We've been united with Christ in his death and resurrection (2:20). And when we died with him, we died to this world. It no longer has any power over us. Christians are never going to be socially respectable. For our boast is the cross—the ultimate symbol of shame. And once you've died to the world, it can no longer bring any social pressure to bear. What it thinks is meaningless to us now. All that counts is a new creation.

We can decide what shapes our sense of what is "normal," "good," and "sensible." Psalm 1 warns us not to "sit in the seat of scoffers" (1:1) but instead to "meditate" on God's Word "day and night" (1:2). Review your reading, viewing, and surfing habits. Do you sit in front of the television or with your tablet in the company of people who mock the truth? What shapes your sense of what's "normal"? Count the hours you spend on the internet, and compare this with the hours you spend in the company of God's Word and Christians who speak the truth.

Perhaps the invitation of Philippians 4:8 has never been more needed:

> Finally, brothers, whatever is true, whatever is honorable, whatever is just, whatever is pure, whatever is lovely, whatever is commendable, if there is any excellence, if there is anything worthy of praise, think about these things.

Finally, don't miss the good news of Scripture alone. God the Father has revealed his love in the person of his Son, and through the Spirit we have that revelation in our hands. And Scripture is not just the touchstone for the truth. God gave us the Scriptures so we might enter into a relationship with him. William Tyndale wrote,

> The scripture is that wherewith God draweth us unto him. . . . The scriptures spring out of God, and flow unto Christ, and were given to lead us to Christ. Thou must therefore go along by the scripture as by a line, until thou come at Christ, which is the way's end and resting-place.[6]

Reflection Questions

1. Imagine not having the Bible in a language you could read. What difference would that make to you day to day?
2. From what sources do people today get their opinions?
3. What do you think are the main threats to *Scripture alone* today?
4. What parts of the Bible does our culture find hard to accept?
5. What should we do when we interpret the Bible differently?
6. Identify a recent occasion when the Bible led you to rest or joy in Christ.

Getting Personal

1. What parts of the Bible do you find hard to accept?
2. What do you do with these issues?
3. Audit your reading, watching, listening, and surfing. What are the dominant influences on your thoughts and attitudes?

Voices of the Reformation: The Clarity of the Word of God

Each chapter ends with an extended quotation so that we hear the authentic voice of the Reformation. Our first extract is from Huldrych Zwingli, the leader of the Reformation in Zurich. In 1522, he preached to a convent. The nuns were persuaded, and the convent closed. His sermon was published as "The Clarity and Certainty of the Word of God." In it, Zwingli is responding to the argument that because there are different interpretations of the Bible, we need the Catholic Church to tell which is correct. He argues for the clarity of the Bible's central message and gives guidelines for distinguishing between true and false interpretations.

> The Word of God is so sure and strong that, if God wills, all things are done the moment that he speaks his Word. . . .
>
> When the Word of God shines on the human understanding, it enlightens it in such a way that it understands and confesses the Word and knows the certainty of it. This was the inner experience of David, and he spoke of it in Psalm 119: "The entrance of thy words, O Lord, giveth light; it giveth understanding unto the simple," meaning, those who in themselves are nothing, resembling the child whom Jesus set in the midst of his disciples to teach them humility (Matt. 18). . . .
>
> Those who defend the doctrines of men say . . . if there is a conflict between your understanding and ours, someone will have to decide between us and have authority to silence the one who is in error. And this they say in order to subject

the interpretation of God's Word to men. . . . In direct contradiction to the teaching of Paul, that all interpretation and thought and experience should be made captive to the will and service of God, they try to subject the doctrine of God to the judgment of men. . . . Oh you rascals—you are not instructed or versed in the Gospel, and you pick out verses from it without regard to their context, and wrest them according to your own desire. It is like breaking off a flower from its roots and trying to plant it in a garden. But that is not the way: you must plant it with the roots and the soil in which it is embedded. And similarly we must leave the Word of God its own proper nature if its sense is to be the same to all of us. And those who err in this way we can easily vanquish by leading them back to the source, though they never come willingly. . . .

Even popes and councils have sometimes fallen into serious error, especially Anastasius, and Liberius in the Arian heresy. Will you concede that? Yes. Then your case is lost, for you must allow that if they erred once there is always the fear that they will err again, and therefore we cannot trust in them with any certainty. Once we have discovered that—for . . . all men are liars, deceiving and being deceived—we see that ultimately only God himself can teach us the truth with such certainty that all doubts are removed.[7]

2

HOW TO KNOW GOD'S APPROVAL

The Reforming Joy of Faith Alone in Christ Alone (Galatians 2)

How can I gain God's approval? How can I be right with God so that I enjoy his love and escape his judgment? This question is the key to finding true joy. Indeed, it's the most important question in the world. At stake is our eternal future. Yet in an act of staggering negligence, most people put it out of their minds.

Not so young Luther. In his early life, whenever he heard the phrase "the righteousness of God," his thoughts were filled with dread. The two English words *righteousness* and *justice* both translate the same Greek word. Consequently, when Luther thought about God's righteousness, he immediately thought of God as a judge executing justice. So he kept going to confession. He quickly gained a reputation for his devotion and duty. Yet he could find no peace or forgiveness or hope. How could he? He knew he didn't measure up. He knew that when he faced God's perfect justice, he would be condemned. There was no joy in the righteousness of God. Or so he thought.

Faith Alone in Christ Alone in the Reformation

At the heart of the Reformation was the issue of justification. And this is what it means: it's the act whereby we become right with God, righteous, in the right. It anticipates a "not guilty" verdict when we stand before God on the day of judgment.

There were two breakthrough moments for Luther. The first was when he realized that the righteousness of God is not just a *characteristic* of God (that he judges justly) but also a *gift* from God. God gives righteousness.

This was not particularly new. Every good medieval Catholic believed in God's grace. But they believed grace was a spiritual boost that God gave to help us live a life that he would count as righteous. We might not reach 100 percent, but God in his grace might lower the pass mark. If you did enough good deeds, then he would use them to cancel out your sin. To help us, we receive grace through baptism and Communion as a kind of shot of spiritual caffeine to boost our spiritual performance. So there's lots of talk of grace. But there's no room for assurance. God's grace is a power that helps you, perhaps, maybe, on a good day, be good enough for him. No peace, no access, no hope.

Luther's second breakthrough moment was when he realized that God's righteousness is not just a boost to help us become righteous. First and foremost, it's the declaration that we are righteous.

The Catholic Church said that righteousness is "imparted" as a power to help us live a good life. The Reformers said that Christ's righteousness is "imputed" to us, that is, "counted" or "considered." God counts us righteous in Christ. In ourselves we are unrighteous and therefore condemned, but in Christ we are righteous and therefore justified.

So God's grace is not a spiritual boost. In fact, it's not a "thing" at all but an attitude of God—his undeserved love. What we deserve is condemnation. But God in his love condemns Christ in our place, and we receive Christ's righteousness in return. One of Luther's favorite ways of describing this was as a marriage. We're like a poor, disgraced woman who marries a prince:

> Faith unites us with Christ in the same way that a bride is united with her husband. As a result everything they have, they now hold in common, the good as well as the evil. So we glory in whatever Christ has as though it were ours. And whatever we have, Christ now claims as his own. And if we compare this exchange then we shall see benefits that cannot be calculated. Christ is full of grace, life and salvation. The soul is full of sins, death and damnation. Now let faith come between Christ and us. Our sins, death and damnation now belong to Christ, while his grace, life and salvation are now ours. For if Christ is a husband, he must take on himself the things which belong to his bride. And he must give to her the things that are his. Not only that, he also gives us himself.[1]

So God's declaration that we're righteous is not something that *may* happen, *perhaps*, if we're good enough. Rather, by faith we can be confident that we'll be declared not guilty on the day of judgment. Indeed, that future declaration has already taken place in the resurrection of Jesus:

> [Christ] was delivered up for our trespasses and raised for our justification.
>
> Therefore, since we have been justified by faith, we have peace with God through our Lord Jesus Christ. Through him we have also obtained access by faith into this grace in which we stand, and we rejoice in hope of the glory of God. (Rom. 4:25–5:2)

So justification is not something we do at all. Luther talks about it as "passive righteousness." It's passive from our perspective—we contribute nothing. It's not merely a boost to our efforts. Everything needed is done by Christ, and as a result, we have peace, access, and hope.

The essence of the Reformation is often summarized as five *solas*, from the Latin word meaning "sole" or "alone." The five are Scripture alone, Christ alone, faith alone, grace alone, and God's glory alone. We've met *Scripture alone* already. Now we see that we are saved in *Christ alone* by *grace alone* through *faith alone*. And because God does everything, we can't claim any credit, so it's to *God's glory alone*.

Did Luther Get It Wrong?

So far so good. But Luther has been accused of two things.

First, he has been accused of imposing his own angst on the message of the New Testament. Luther, so the argument goes, was plagued by an uneasy conscience. The more Freudian version speculates that he had a bad relationship with his father (certainly, his father wanted him to be a lawyer and was disappointed when Luther became a monk). So according to this accusation, Luther was so desperate for peace of mind that he grabbed hold of one idea and made it central to Christianity.

But I believe Luther's state of mind is irrelevant. Maybe he had a bad relationship with his father. Maybe he was full of angst. Maybe he was a man of his times, terrified by the lurid, doom-laden paintings that covered the walls of medieval churches.

But the point is this: before God we're all objectively guilty because we've all sinned. Luther felt this deeply, and it weighed him down. But whether people feel it or not, it's true. What Luther rediscovered in justification by faith was God's solution to this problem. Humanity's greatest problem was matched by God's greatest solution.

Second, Luther has been accused of imposing the situation he faced in the sixteenth century on the very different situation Paul faced in the first century. To return to our analogy of a time machine, Luther forgot where his time machine was. This is one of the claims made by what's known as "the New Perspective on Paul."[2] Luther, so the argument goes, faced people who claimed that we're saved by works, and he wrongly assumed that Paul had faced the same challenge.

Now there's something to this argument. The presenting question in Galatia was indeed "Who belongs to God's people?" rather than "How are we saved?" But this accusation misreads medieval Catholicism. Catholicism didn't claim that we're saved by works—not quite. Every baptized baby receives God's grace. But then our works, combined with fill-ups of grace, ensure that we continue to be righteous. And that's actually pretty close to what was going on in Galatia.

This accusation also doesn't do justice to Paul. The presenting issue might be who belongs in the church, but Paul keeps bringing it back to how we're saved. "You can't claim we're saved by faith," he argues, "and then claim people need to be circumcised to be part of God's people. Once you start down that line, you undermine faith alone in Christ alone":

> Look: I, Paul, say to you that if you accept circumcision, Christ will be of no advantage to you. I testify again to every man who accepts circumcision that he is obligated to keep the whole law. You are severed from Christ, you who would be justified by the law; you have fallen away from grace. (Gal. 5:2–4)

Luther describes the law as "a complete package; you cannot take one part of it and ignore the rest."[3] Once you start saying that Christians are *acceptable* by keeping the law, then you should go the whole way and say we're *justified* by the law—in which case your faith is in your works and Christ is of no value. And once you say that *one* commandment is needed, then logically every commandment must be obeyed. By this point, your salvation is wrecked. The gospel is not the ABC of Christianity with the law supplying D to Z. The gospel is the A to Z of Christianity.[4]

Faith Alone in Christ Alone in Galatia

In Galatians 2:11–14, Paul describes how, under pressure from "the circumcision group," the apostle Peter had stopped eating with Gentiles ("Cephas" is the Aramaic form of "Peter"). Eating a meal with someone is a powerful symbol of acceptance—then and now. And "the circumcision group" wouldn't accept Gentile believers until they had been circumcised. Perhaps there was a racist element to this—a sense of racial superiority. But more importantly, it was a religious issue. "You may be saved by faith, but you belong by circumcision," they said. "You may start by faith, but you continue by keeping the law."

Paul confronted the apostle Peter. That's a big deal. Peter was the leader of the apostles. He had accompanied Jesus. He had been given his nickname Peter, meaning "rock," by Jesus. His confession of faith was the foundation of the church (Matt. 16:15–18). But now "the rock" was crumbling, and the victim was joy.

Paul told Peter, "If you, though a Jew, live like a Gentile and not like a Jew, how can you force the Gentiles to live like Jews?" (Gal. 2:14). Peter used to believe that the Jews were God's exclusive people and that keeping the law was the mark of salvation. Not anymore—not since he had met Jesus. Now he knew that he was saved by faith in Christ. So now he lived "like a Gentile and not like a Jew." In other words, he didn't offer sacrifices in the temple or keep the food laws of Moses. He saw all those pictures fulfilled in Christ, our true sacrifice and temple. Peter's new life was a testimony to the fact that salvation is by faith in Christ. And so it made no sense at all for Peter to insist that other people be circumcised. If Peter was a Jew who now acted like a Gentile, then why make Gentiles act like Jews? Paul continues in 2:15–16:

> We ourselves are Jews by birth and not Gentile sinners; yet we know that a person is not justified by works of the law but through faith in Jesus Christ, so we also have believed in Christ Jesus, in order to be justified by faith in Christ and not by works of the law, because by works of the law no one will be justified.

The "we" here are Jewish Christians—people who are "Jews by birth" but who have now put their "faith in Jesus Christ." Paul is appealing to a common understanding. "We all know this," he says. "I don't need to tell you this or prove this to you. We know we're justified by faith and not by the law. We Jews learned this lesson the hard way. We had God's law, God's king, God's prophets. But we couldn't make ourselves righteous. More than anyone, we should know that people can't reform their lives or erase their guilt." Again, 2:16 says, "A person is not justified by works of the law . . . not by works of the law. . . . By works of the law no one will be justified." Three times we're told the same thing: not by works, not by works, not by works.

The reason why we reject this message is that it humbles us. We don't want to be told that we're helpless. Somewhere along the line we want to feel like our efforts make a difference. Irreligious people reject Jesus because they don't want Jesus to be their *Lord*—they want to run their own lives. But religious people also reject him. They don't want Jesus to be their *Savior*. They cling to the notion that—yes, with a bit of help from God—they can sort out their lives. But God says, "By works of the law no one will be justified."

So what can we do? Again, 2:16 says, "A person is . . . justified . . . through faith in Jesus Christ. . . . We also have believed in Christ Jesus, in order to be justified by faith in Christ." Again, three times we're told: faith in Christ, faith in Christ, faith in Christ. It's really a way of saying that we do nothing and Christ does everything.

Talk of *faith alone* can be a bit misleading. I watched a television program recently in which the presenter kept talking about faith: "I don't have faith but admire people who do have faith." "Faith can be a great comfort." He had badly missed the point. Faith is not a "thing" you have, find, keep, or lose. It's a relational bond. It's trust in something else. And it's that something else that matters. Faith in the tooth fairy is not much use because—spoiler alert—tooth fairies don't exist. Before you step onto a bridge, you need to trust that it will take your weight. That's faith. When the Reformers emphasized faith alone, it wasn't because faith itself is virtuous, somehow earning merit with God. It was because faith connects us to Christ. Faith is letting go of self-confidence (what Paul calls "the flesh") and entrusting yourself entirely to Christ. So the Reformation emphasis on *faith alone* was a way of directing the focus onto Christ and his finished work. Catholicism said the sacraments and religious duties connect you to Christ, thereby smuggling good works back into the picture. But whenever you hear the words *faith alone*, you must also think *Christ alone*. Faith alone connects us to Christ, and Christ alone saves.

Christ is complete and perfect in his life, love, patience, compassion, anger, justice, kindness. He's perfect in his words, thoughts, and actions. He's perfect in his love for God and his love for people. He's the Righteous One. Yet he died, the righteous for the unrighteous, bearing the judgment of God. He was made sin for us, treated as a sinner in our place. And his death was complete. It covered all our sin.

"If righteousness were through the law," Paul says in 2:21, "then Christ died for no purpose." The very fact that Jesus had to die shows that there is no other way of salvation. If you think your works contribute to your acceptance by God, then in effect you're saying, "Thank you for dying for me, Jesus, but your death wasn't enough. I need to top it off." But Christ's death *was* complete, and there's nothing left for us to do. The African American preacher D. J. Ward puts it like this:

> "His name shall be called Jesus, for he shall save . . ." Not attempt to save. Not try to save. Not hope to save. Not want to save. But "he shall save his people from their sins." Now I hear this—I hear it on televisions, I hear it in churches—that

> God has done all he can do, the rest is up to you. If the rest is up to you, then he didn't accomplish it. . . . But if he did do it, he doesn't need your best and your works need not speak for you. If he did do it, you can leave here rejoicing. . . . He paid it all—every drop of it.[5]

The gospel makes us small and Christ big.

Faith Alone in Christ Alone in Our World

Everyone is trying to find salvation. They might not ask, "What must I do to be saved?" But everyone has some sense of what would make them satisfied, fulfilled, accepted. People define it in many different ways: eternal life, success in business, a beautiful home, being adored by others, a liberated homeland, a secure future, acceptance, family. Everyone has something that they would like to be or have or do—something that, if achieved, would make life complete.

But these versions of salvation don't deliver. The novels of Jack Higgins have sold over 250 million copies, yet Higgins said, "I wish I had known that when you make it to the top, there is nothing there."[6] King Solomon said much the same thing. Despite achieving great power, wealth, and wisdom, he concluded, "All is vanity" (Eccles. 1:2). These things don't deliver because we were made for more. We may find some measure of success, but our hearts are always restless until they find rest in God.[7]

And with every version of salvation comes a rule or a law: "I will get salvation if I . . ." If your idea of salvation is being accepted by friends, then your rule will be "Thou shalt be cool." If your idea of salvation is a beautiful home, then your Bible will be *Better Homes and Gardens* magazine. Your rule will be vintage furniture, tiled floors, and distressed paint or clean lines, white walls, and no clutter. If you want to be adored by the opposite sex, then you'll have a list of dietary rules, an exercise regimen, a style guide. It may not be the law of Moses. But everyone is trying to be justified by works of the law.

There are big differences between all these "laws." But what they all have in common is this: "I did it my way." This line comes from the most commonly played song at funerals, "My Way," popularized by Frank Sinatra. This is how humanity lives, and this is how humanity faces death: "my way."

So Galatians speaks to our culture and our friends. Everyone lives by a set of rules designed to achieve his or her personal version of "righteous." People want to justify or prove themselves. But "by works of the law no one will be justified," says Galatians 2:16. Doing it "my way" doesn't work. In 3:4, Paul says, "Did you suffer so many things in vain?" Suffer indeed. Self-justification is hard work. It takes dedication and sacrifice. And then it gets you nowhere.

It's all so insecure because you're only ever as good as your latest performance. If you want to be admired by men, but you're not manly enough, then you're condemned. If you want prosperity and you lose your job, then you're devastated. When you don't measure up, then your "god" turns on you and curses you. Your law condemns you. You're a failure. And in the end all our versions of salvation run into the buffers of death. Death is the great wrecking ball of self-justification and self-fulfillment.

The good news is that there's a truer, better version of salvation. We can be right with God and find joy in him. And there's nothing bigger or better than God, the ultimate source of all joy. And what happens when we don't measure up? "Christ redeemed us from the curse of the law by becoming a curse for us" (3:13). Instead of our "god" condemning us, Jesus is condemned in our place.

Faith Alone in Christ Alone in Our Churches

How did you first become a Christian (if you are one)? Remind yourself of the story. Now ask yourself this: Did I become a Christian after I sorted my life out or by putting my faith in Christ? That's Paul's challenge to the Galatians in Galatians 3:2–3: "Let me ask you only this: Did you receive the Spirit by works of the law or by hearing with faith? Are you so foolish? Having begun by the Spirit, are you now being perfected by the flesh?" We all have different conversion stories. Some are dramatic, some gradual. Many of us struggle to name a date. But common to them all is faith in Christ. Salvation is not something we achieved. All we did was reach out to receive it as a gift from God.

Our problem is that we all too easily forget this. We forget that we received the Spirit through faith and not as a reward for our works. We forget that left to ourselves, we were powerless to change. And so we go back to our old ways. We start trying to live the Christian life "my way." We try to be acceptable Christians by keeping a law. We think what makes us righteous is attending the prayer meeting, being able to quote Bible verses, leading a moral life, or responding emotionally in corporate worship. Our prayers or our tears, we think, make us acceptable Christians. Then we look down on people who don't measure up to our standards. Or we become anxious when we don't measure up. We live like slaves instead of sons.

The Galatians are returning to legalism and losing their joy. So this is an invitation to rediscover joy. If your life lacks joy, then this is for you. I don't mean being happy all the time—sometimes life is painful. But even in those moments we will find comfort in God. If you can't find that comfort or if you've lost your fizz, then listen up. Here's a diagnostic for a lack of spiritual zest.

We Lose Our Joy When We Use Religious Duty to Impress Others

It's not clear whether Peter agreed with those who said that Gentiles should be circumcised. But either way, he went along with them, "fearing the circumcision party" (Gal. 2:12). He wanted to be with the in-crowd. And this was also what was happening in Galatia. The Gentile Christians were being forced to return to religion to fit in.

I wonder what you do, not because it's the right thing to do or because you want to please God but because you fear the disapproval of other people.

- If you come to a prayer meeting because you feel the need to pray or because you love talking with God, then you'll have a great time. But if you come to a prayer meeting because you fear disapproval, then it'll feel like a burden. And there'll be no joy.
- If you show hospitality because you love people, then you'll have a great time—even if you're left with a messy house. But if you show hospitality because you feel you must or to impress other people, then it'll feel like a burden. And there'll be no joy.
- If you share the gospel because you're passionate about Jesus, then you'll do so with infectious enthusiasm. But if you share the gospel because you want to impress people with your stories at the prayer meeting, then it'll feel like a burden. And there'll be no joy.

This is why some people have a low capacity for service. It's because service has become a burden, and none of us can carry a burden for long. Sooner or later we need to stop and recover. But Jesus says, "My yoke is easy, and my burden is light" (Matt. 11:30). If the burden of serving Christ feels heavy, then something is wrong. The chances are that you're trying to prove yourself or impress others.

We Lose Our Joy When We Use Religious Duty to Control Sin

"Yes, we all agree that we're justified by faith. But we need religious duties to grow as Christians." That's the objection Paul anticipates in Galatians 2:17. This is how he puts it: "But if, in our endeavor to be justified in Christ, we too were found to be sinners, is Christ then a servant of sin?" First-century Jews divided the world into righteous Jews and sinful Gentiles. If Christians weren't among the righteous Jews as defined by circumcision, then they must be among the sinners. And if not now, then surely that's where they would end up without the law to keep them on track. It's a powerful argument. When Christians struggle with sin, they're tempted to revert to a law. Or when we see other people sinning, we're tempted to impose a law on them.

But Paul will have none of it. "Certainly not!" he says (2:17). That's because the law can only *expose* sin. It can't stop it or cure it. We shouldn't rebuild what we tore down (2:18). In other words, we shouldn't reintroduce religious duty as a way of life, having rejected it as a way of conversion. If you reimpose the law, then all you'll do is turn people into lawbreakers. The law was supposed to point us to Christ. You undermine that purpose if, having found Christ, you then walk away from him and back to it. Indeed, in an unexpected twist, that actually makes you the ultimate lawbreaker, because you act contrary to the law's true purpose (2:18). For you're walking away from Christ rather than toward him. Luther says,

> Although the law discloses and increases sin, it is not against the promises of God but for them. The reason for this is that

> it humbles us and prepares us to seek for grace. . . . When the law forces us to acknowledge and confess our sins in this way it has fulfilled its function and is no longer needed, because the moment for grace has come.[8]

It was only when I gave up trying to *earn* God's approval that I could *receive* God's approval by faith (2:19). When I was trying to earn approval, my motives were confused. I was trying to please God, but what I really cared about was my salvation. Only when I received salvation as a gift could I truly make pleasing God my focus.

So What Happens Next?

If it's not by law, then how do we live and grow as Christians? We need to realize that becoming a Christian is not just a change of opinion or a lifestyle choice. It's a death and resurrection. You die to your old life, and you live a new life. At this point you might be saying, "Hang on a moment. I think I would have noticed if I had died!" But Paul says we died and rose *in Christ* when Christ was crucified and resurrected: "I have been crucified with Christ. It is no longer I who live, but Christ who lives in me" (Gal. 2:20). Before Christ we had no innate desire or ability to please God. But now we've been remade. Now what's innate is Christ! "Christ lives in me." Calvin says, "Engrafted into the death of Christ, we derive a secret energy from it, as the shoot does from the root."[9]

What does this look like in practice? Galatians 2:20 continues: "And the life I now live in the flesh I live by faith in the Son of God, who loved me and gave himself for me." What *now motivates* us is "faith in the Son of God." This is our drive, our passion, our enthusiasm. It's not just faith in some abstract truth or theological dogma; it's much more personal. It's faith in the one "who loved me and gave himself for me." His love leads to our love. His sacrifice leads to our sacrifice.

Paul says, "It was before your eyes that Jesus Christ was publicly portrayed as crucified" (3:1). He's saying, "We proclaimed Christ so clearly, it was as if you could see him for yourselves." That's how we help one another—not by imposing a set of rules but by portraying Christ crucified. Our mantra is "The Son of God loved you and gave himself for you." And that produces lives characterized by drive, passion, and enthusiasm. Even in the midst of service and sacrifice, it creates lives of joy.

Reflection Questions

1. Think about the people you know. How might they complete these sentences?

   I'll be happy, fulfilled, accepted if . . .
   The people I look up to are . . .
   To achieve this, I have to . . .
   When I fall short of my rules, I . . .

   The first two sentences reveal how they define salvation. The third sentence reveals the law or rules they follow. The fourth exposes what happens when they themselves don't measure up. What about you? How would you complete these sentences?

2. Complete the sentences above with a gospel answer using the language of Galatians.
3. How does living by faith turn things we ought to do into things we want to do?

Getting Personal

1. When does service feel like a burden to you?

2. What gospel motives are there for the service that currently feels like a burden to you?
3. How will these lead to joy?
4. Insert your name into Galatians 2:20:

> "The life _________ now lives in the flesh, _________ lives by faith in the Son of God, who loved _________ and gave himself for _________."

Voices of the Reformation: Active and Passive Righteousness

As we have seen, lecturing on Galatians was one of the key factors in reshaping Luther's thought. In the preface to his commentary on Galatians, he describes two different kinds of righteousness: active and passive. Active righteousness is our obedience to God's law, civic laws, and social norms. These are all good because they show how to behave and maintain an orderly society. But we must never let them govern our conscience, because they can never make us right before God. For that we need passive righteousness—passive because we don't do anything except receive it from Christ by faith. The problem is that in our pride we keep slipping back into thinking that we contribute to our approval before God. But when we do that, we quickly begin to despair. Our only hope is to go back again and again to the righteousness of Christ. Indeed, only then can we truly love others without that love being a selfish attempt to win God's approval.

> So then, do we do nothing to obtain this righteousness? No, nothing at all. Perfect righteousness is to do nothing, to hear nothing, to know nothing of the law or of works, but to know

and believe only that Christ has gone to the Father and is no longer visible; that he sits in heaven at the right hand of his Father, not as a judge, but is made by God our wisdom, righteousness, holiness, and redemption; in short that he is our high priest, entreating for us and reigning over us and in us by grace. . . .

Therefore, St. Paul, in this letter, teaches us in order to comfort us and to confirm us in the perfect knowledge of this most Christian and excellent righteousness, for once we lose our belief in justification, all true Christian doctrine is lost. There is no middle ground between the righteousness of the law and Christian righteousness. Anyone who strays from Christian righteousness must fall into the righteousness of the law; in other words, when people lose Christ, they slip back into reliance on their own works.

That is why we so earnestly repeat this doctrine of faith or Christian righteousness, so that it may be continually exercised and may be plainly distinguished from the active righteousness of the law. Otherwise we should never be able to believe the true theology. The church is founded on, and consists in, this doctrine alone. So if we want to teach and lead other people, we need to pay careful attention to these matters and to note well this distinction between the righteousness of the law and the righteousness of Christ. This is easy to describe in words but hard to put into practice, for when we are near death or in other agonies of conscience these two sorts of righteousness come closer together than we would wish. . . .

Let us then be careful to learn to discriminate between these two kinds of righteousness, so that we may know how far we should obey the law. We have already seen that for a Christian the law ought to have dominion only over the flesh. When it is so, the law is kept within bounds. But if it presumes to creep into your conscience and tries to reign there, you must make the right distinction. Give no more to the law than is right, but say, "You want to climb up into the kingdom of my conscience, do you, Law? You want to reign over it and reprove sin and take away the joy I have by faith in Christ and drive me to desperation? Keep within your bounds, and exercise your power over the flesh, but do not touch my conscience. By the Gospel I am called to share righteousness and everlasting life. I am called to Christ's kingdom, where my conscience is at rest and there is no law, but rather forgiveness of sins, peace, quietness, joy, health, and everlasting life. Do not trouble me in these matters, for I will not let an intolerable tyrant like you reign in my conscience, which is the temple of Christ, the Son of God. He is the King of righteousness and peace, my sweet Savior and Mediator; he will keep my conscience joyful and quiet in the sound, pure doctrine of the Gospel and in the knowledge of Christian and heavenly righteousness."

When I have this righteousness reigning in my heart, I descend from heaven like the rain that makes the earth fertile. That is to say, I come out into another kingdom, and I do good works whenever I have a chance. If I am a minister of the Word, I preach, I comfort the brokenhearted, I administer the sacraments. If I am a householder, I am in charge of my house and my family, and I bring up my children in the knowledge and fear of God. If I am a magistrate, I work hard at the job that heaven has given me. If I am a servant, I do my master's business faithfully. Whoever is convinced that Christ is his righteousness works cheerfully and well in his vocation.[10]

3

HOW TO RECOGNIZE GOD'S PEOPLE

The Reforming Joy of Mother Church (Galatians 3–4)

When Luther was excommunicated from the Catholic Church by the pope in 1521, there was nowhere else to go. In Western Europe the Roman Catholic Church was the only show in town. Luther couldn't go down the road to his local Methodist church or an independent evangelical church. There was only one church, and he was on the outside.

The response of the Reformers was to rethink what it meant to be a church. Everyone thought of the church as an institution with parish churches across Europe, a hierarchy of clergy and a history dating back to the first apostles. All these might be good to have, the Reformers said, but the key mark of a true church is that it rightly preaches the gospel.

At first, Luther hoped to reform the Catholic Church. But as the church opposed the message of justification by faith, he realized that there was a much bigger problem. Luther knew that every human institution has its faults—he wasn't a starry-eyed idealist. But if a church no longer preaches justification by faith—and in fact actively opposes it, as the Catholic Church was doing—then it can no longer be a true church.

That meant Luther wasn't really leaving the church, because the Catholic Church wasn't a true church. The Reformation was not a schism (a split in the church). It was the re-*formation* of a true church around the true gospel.

We continue to face these issues today. What should you look for in a potential church? Whenever my wife and I have bought a house, we've had a list of four or five things we were looking for. But gradually the realities of our limited budget meant the nonnegotiables on our desirable list reduced until just one or two remained. In the same way, we could perhaps all compile a wish list of the things we'd love to find in a church. A good cup of tea would be on mine. But what really matters? What are the nonnegotiables?

And what about leaving a church? Should you leave if you disagree with a decision of the leaders? If it no longer suits your children? If one of the leaders falls into sin? These are painful issues. You invest so much in a local church that leaving it can feel like a bereavement.

And let's extend the questions beyond your local church. How should you view other churches, especially those with which you disagree? When can you cooperate together? When must you keep your distance? What are we to make of the structures of denominations?

The Reformers said that there are two key marks of a true church: the preaching of the gospel word and the administration of the gospel sacraments. John Calvin, Martin Bucer, and the Anabaptists added a third sign: church discipline—a true church ensures its members are true Christians living in accordance with the gospel (Matt. 16:19; 18:15–20).

The Roman Catholic Church claimed that its hierarchy and history gave it the final authority. It alone had the power to say how the Bible should be interpreted. But the Reformers said that this got things the wrong way round. It's not the church that creates the gospel. It's the gospel that creates the church. The authority over the church is not the pope in Rome or any human hierarchy. The Head is Christ. He's our Husband, our Head, our King. We don't have a secondhand rule. The word *vicar* comes from a Latin noun that means "substitute" (an Anglican vicar was originally a substitute for an absent incumbent). From the eighth century the pope has been called "the vicar of Christ." He is seen as Christ's substitute or representative on earth. But we don't have a substitute husband. Christ himself cares for his church and governs his church by his Spirit through his Word.

The role of preachers and leaders in the church is to proclaim that Word. They have authority to the extent that they rightly teach God's Word—nothing more and nothing less. It's "nothing more" in the sense that the only authority they have is to apply what the Bible says. We can give wise advice as friends, but we can tell people what they must do only when that is clear from the Scriptures. Yet this authority is "nothing less" than the authority of Christ himself. As your pastor preaches God's Word, it is Christ himself who addresses his church. Christ himself brings comfort and challenge through the preaching of his Word.

Defining the Church in First-Century Galatia

Paul faced two big questions as he wrote to the church in Galatia: First, who belongs to the people of God? And second, who has authority over them? Justification by faith is not just a doctrine for me; it radically affects how we view other Christians. This is Paul's main theme in Galatians.

We've seen already that the false teachers believed that Gentiles could be saved by faith but needed to be circumcised to belong to God's people. After all, they said, it's the children of Abraham who are the people of God. How does Paul respond?

"Those Who Have Faith"

First, Paul says that Abraham does indeed define God's people. But what's that definition? "Understand, then, that those who have faith are children of Abraham" (Gal. 3:7 NIV). It's not ethnicity, history, morality, or religion that determines whether you're part of God's people. It's faith. Who are God's people? "Those who have faith."

"Those Who Rely on Faith"

Paul also anticipates an objection: "For hundreds of years God's people were defined by the law. And you, Paul, have suddenly shown up and ditched the law. You can't overturn centuries of history like that with your newfangled innovations."

But Paul says that this is *not* an innovation and he's not making it up as he goes: "Scripture foresaw that God would justify the Gentiles by faith, and announced the gospel in advance to Abraham: 'All nations will be blessed through you.' So those who rely on faith are blessed along with Abraham, the man of faith" (3:8–9 NIV). It was God's plan from the beginning to take people from all nations and make them his children—not by becoming Jewish or keeping the law but through faith. And the coming of the law didn't mean a change of plan. Covenants or contracts don't work like that—not human covenants and certainly not divine ones (3:15–18). God's people have always been defined by faith. Who are God's people? "Those who rely on faith."

Those Who Have Faith in Christ

And God's people have always been defined by faith in Christ. Faith is not some sense of optimism or belief in the spiritual. Saving faith is faith in God's promised Savior. The covenant with Abraham was made with his "seed," or "offspring" (3:16). Paul plays on the ambiguity of that word. It can be a collective term, or it can refer to an individual. Paul says it refers to an individual, Christ. The identity of the collective people of God is defined by an individual, Jesus. He is the focus of the promise. Who are God's people? Those who have faith in Christ.

Unblocking the Pipe

Not only does Israel's history show that God's people are defined by faith, but also when Israel switched track to relying on the law, the result was a disaster: "For all who rely on works of the law are under a curse" (Gal. 3:10). Works don't work! "Curse" here doesn't mean some kind of spooky jinx that brings bad luck. It's much worse than that. It means God's judgment. And for Israel that meant exile. Relying on the law didn't reinforce their identity. It unraveled their identity.

None of us makes the grade. Although we might keep some laws some of the time, no one keeps all the law all the time. But that's actually not the main problem, which is that relying on yourself means not relying on God (3:11–12). It's not just that you break some laws. The whole orientation of your life is a rejection of him. Even when you keep the law, you're doing so in defiance of God. So while some people rebel against God by *breaking* his law, others do so by keeping his law. It's a self-reliant rejection of his help. Luther saw this so clearly. Even as we obey the law, he said, we hate it—along with the God who gave it to us:

> Outwardly you keep the law with works out of fear of punishment or love of gain. . . . You'd rather act otherwise if the law didn't exist. It follows, then, that you, in the depths of your heart, are an enemy of the law. . . . Because in doing such works the heart abhors the law and yet is forced to obey it, the works are a total loss and are completely useless. . . . That is why faith alone makes someone just and fulfils the law; faith it is that brings the Holy Spirit through the merits of Christ. The Spirit, in turn, renders the heart glad and free, as the law demands. Then good works proceed from faith itself.[1]

So sometimes we need to repent of doing the right thing for the wrong reasons—of trying to prove ourselves or rely on ourselves. Sometimes we need to say, "Sorry, Lord, this hasn't been about you. It's been about me and my pride. I've relied on my efforts. I've tried to prove myself. All these good things I've done have really only been to impress other people. And I can't keep it up."

Blessing was supposed to flow to the Gentiles as God's people modeled enjoying God by trusting God (3:8). People were supposed to look on and say, "Wow, that looks brilliant; let's find out more about this God." But when Israel didn't trust God, she became like a blocked pipe. Instead of blessing flowing out to the world, a curse came on her. So Jesus had to unblock the pipe by removing the curse (3:13). He rebooted the people of God, with faith in God back at the center. As a result, he "redeemed us . . . so that in Christ Jesus the blessing of Abraham might come to the Gentiles" (3:13–14). "Us" here means believing Jews. Think of the first Christians. They were all Jews. Christ redeemed them from the curse. What happened next? Filled with God's Spirit, they took the good news to Judea, Samaria, and the ends of the earth. Once again blessing flowed to the world.

This is what's under threat if people like Peter stop eating with Gentile Christians or Gentiles are forced to be circumcised. If we're relying on works, then people will look on and say, "That doesn't look like much fun; Christianity looks like hard work." But as we should know by now, relying on faith leads to joy. Then people are much more likely to say, "Wow, that looks brilliant; let's find out more about their God."

All this begs the question: If the law doesn't identify God's people, then why was it given in the first place? Paul's answer is that the law was designed to lead us to Christ in two ways (2:17–19; 3:19–25):

- In history by testifying to him before his coming
- In our personal experience by revealing our need for a Savior

A Whistle-Stop Tour

Every step of the way, Paul's argument has been that what defines the church is the gospel and that what defines those who belong to the church is faith in the gospel.

Let's jump back in our time machine and do a whistle-stop tour to see how these principles play out. First stop: first-century Galatia. The climax of Paul's argument is this:

> For in Christ Jesus you are all sons of God, through faith. For as many of you as were baptized into Christ have put on

> Christ. There is neither Jew nor Greek, there is neither slave nor free, there is no male and female, for you are all one in Christ Jesus. And if you are Christ's, then you are Abraham's offspring, heirs according to promise. (Gal. 3:26–29)

In the church there is "neither Jew nor Greek" (3:28). It's not that those identities disappear. You can still be proud of your Jewish or English or Italian heritage. But they don't define who is part of God's people. Who are the children of God? Those who belong to Christ by faith (3:29).

Second stop: sixteenth-century Europe. The Roman Catholic Church said that history and hierarchy defined the true church. If you stepped out of this institution, then you stepped out of the true church and therefore out of salvation. But the Reformers, basing their theology on Paul, said that *the gospel* defines the church. The marks of the church are gospel preaching and gospel sacraments.

Third stop: your church. Hierarchy and history matter. Churches have to be organized. Denominations, associations, and partnerships provide a sense of belonging beyond my local church and create opportunities for cooperation. But they're not what define the church. When it comes to choosing a church, the key question is, Does it faithfully preach the gospel word? If this is not the case, then you should think twice about joining that church—no matter how entertaining its preachers or wonderful its music or comprehensive its youth program may be. It also means you should think twice about leaving a church that's faithfully preaching the gospel.

Cooperation beyond the Local Church

Side by side in Galatians we have a strong call for dissociation and a strong call for association.

First, we dissociate from everyone who rejects faith alone in Christ alone. Paul says, "If anyone is preaching to you a gospel contrary to the one you received, let him be accursed" (Gal. 1:9). Some people say love is more important than doctrine. But Paul calls down curses on those who espouse false doctrine! Why? Because pitting love against doctrine creates a false dichotomy. Just as love doesn't let people wander down a path that leads over a cliff, so love doesn't let people follow a gospel that is "really no gospel at all" (1:7 NIV).

It's not just right belief that Paul pursues relentlessly; right action matters too. Paul opposes Peter because he's not acting "in step with the truth of the gospel" (2:14). That takes guts. Few people like confrontation. But leaders who refuse to confront error allow great harm to befall the church. Peter's problem wasn't a lack of knowledge. He had received a vision from God mandating him to eat previously unclean food with unclean people (Acts 10–11). His problem was a lack of courage: he "fear[ed] the circumcision party" (Gal. 2:12). We can't afford to put the goal of pleasing people before the goal of serving Christ (1:10).

Second, we associate with everyone who has faith alone in Christ alone. Perhaps you look at other churches with critical eyes. But how does God view them? He sees their faults (along with yours). But above all he sees them wrapped up in Christ's righteousness, and so he loves to bless them. Theological differences may limit how much we can cooperate. But all who are in Christ are brothers and sisters.

I'm deeply aware of my sin and count it a great wonder that God should delight in me because I'm righteous in Christ. So why do I resent God's blessing on others? We need to believe justification by faith not only for ourselves but for others as well. Satan sees their faults and makes their faults the focus of his attention, which leads to accusation. God sees their faults and makes Christ the focus of his attention, which leads to affirmation. And we should be more like God than like Satan!

Who Has Authority over the People of God?

"The mother and head of all the churches in Rome and all the world." These are the words written over the door of the Archbasilica of Saint John Lateran in Rome. This was the first church to be built after the Emperor Constantine made Christianity legal across the Roman Empire. It became the "seat," or base, of the pope. There was a period in the Middle Ages when a number of popes relocated to Avignon in France. During this time the Archbasilica was damaged by fire, and although it was repaired, when the popes returned to Rome, it was deemed inadequate. So the current Saint Peter's Basilica was built together with the Vatican, and these buildings have been the functional center of Catholicism ever since. But the Archbasilica of Saint John remains the official seat of the pope. You don't need a time machine to read the words "The mother and head of all the churches." You just need a ticket to Rome and a Latin dictionary. These words remain the claim of the Catholic Church: here is mother church.

It's very similar to the claims being made by Paul's opponents in Galatia. They expected the Galatians to roll over and do what they said. It's unlikely that they had the official backing of the Jerusalem church (Gal. 2:9), but they spoke as if they did. "You Gentiles should listen to us," they said. "Our church in Jerusalem is larger, stronger, older. We have a long history stretching back to Abraham. The gospel came to you from us. We're your mother church, and we just want to look after our children." They assumed that the Jerusalem church had authority over other churches—after all, it had hierarchy and history on its side. It was a very similar argument to that made later by the Roman Catholic Church.

Think how that sounds today: "You Albanian or African or Afghan Christians ought to listen to us American Christians. Our church in the US is larger, stronger, older. We have a long history stretching back to the Pilgrims. The gospel came to you from us. We're your mother church, and we just want to look after our converts." No one says it quite like that, but that can be the subtext of the way some Western Christians relate to others in the world.

It's easy to congratulate ourselves for not being under the authority of the pope. But we need to be careful not to create our own authorities. Paul invests a lot of energy in maintaining the unity of the church, but he wants a partnership *of equals*.

In Galatians 3, Paul says that the true children of Abraham are those who share his faith. In 4:21–31, he approaches the issue from another angle. He reminds us that Abraham had two children. When Abraham's wife, Sarah, was childless, she suggested that Abraham should sleep with one of her servants, Hagar. But when Hagar became pregnant with Ishmael, she despised Sarah, and Sarah mistreated her. Only when Sarah was nearly ninety did she herself conceive and give birth to Isaac as God had promised. Paul isn't saying that Sarah was more virtuous than Hagar (she wasn't). Instead, they represent two different ways of being God's people: self-reliance (what Paul calls trusting "the flesh") and trusting God's promise. Paul has turned the tables on his opponents: they're like Abraham's child but not the child of promise.

The issue, however, is not just who belongs to God's people but also who has authority over them. Paul says that when people from Jerusalem tell you to be circumcised, they're symbolically from Mount Sinai, where Israel received the law. They're not being motherly. Quite the opposite. They're being like a strict "guardian" who wants to hold you "captive under the law" (3:23–25).

There is a mother church to which we should look and to which we submit. But it's not in Jerusalem or Rome or London—it's in heaven. "But the Jerusalem above is free, and she is our mother," says Paul in 4:26.

This is not just a rhetorical flourish. It speaks right into the issues that the church in Galatia was facing. The people from Jerusalem were telling them to submit because they came from the mother church. But there's no hierarchy: every local church is an expression of the heavenly church with Christ as its head, exercising his authority through his Word.

Finally, don't miss the good news of "mother church." There are lots of Renaissance paintings showing Mary squeezing her breasts so her milk falls to the people below. It's a powerful image of the way we're nurtured by spiritual milk. But that milk doesn't come from the intercessions of Mary. The church gives us birth and nurtures us through preaching God's Word. Peter says we were "born again . . . through the living and abiding word of God," and we grow through "the pure spiritual milk" of God's Word (1 Pet. 1:23; 2:2). God has given you your church as a place where your spiritual life can be nurtured. Luther says,

> The heavenly Jerusalem is the church, that is to say, believers scattered throughout the world, who have the same gospel, the same faith in Christ, the same Holy Spirit and

the same sacraments. This church goes on giving birth to children until the end of the world as long as she exercises the ministry of the Word, for this is what it means for her to give birth.[2]

Reflection Questions

1. Can you think of examples of having to repent of doing the right thing for the wrong reasons?
2. If you were joining a new church, what would be on your wish list? Organize your list from the most important to the least important.
3. Can you think of examples of when it's right to dissociate from other Christians? Can you think of examples of when it's wrong to dissociate?
4. Can you think of examples of one church or one group of Christians trying to exercise authority over another church or group?
5. How is the church like a mother? What comfort is there in knowing that we have a "mother church" in heaven?

Getting Personal

1. Think of another church near you, one that perhaps feels like a "rival." Complete this sentence: "They have faith in Christ, but . . ." What matters most—what comes *before* the word "but" or what comes *after*? What matters most to God?
2. Identify someone in your church who you struggle to get along with. Satan sees that person's faults and makes those faults the focus of his attention. God sees that person's faults and makes Christ the focus of his attention. What difference would it make if your focus were more like God's than Satan's?

Voices of the Reformation: Mother Church

John Calvin was the leader of the Reformation in Geneva who had a genius for presenting Christian truth in a systematic way. Although they left the Catholic Church, the Reformers remained strongly committed to the church and its visible expression in local congregations, as this extract from Calvin's *Institutes of the Christian Religion* shows. We live in a generation that emphasizes individual freedom, and this affects people's attitudes toward their church. For Calvin, in contrast, we are embedded in the communal life of the local church.

> Because it is now our intention to discuss the visible church, let us learn even from the simple title "mother" how useful, indeed how necessary, it is that we should know her. For there is no other way to enter into life unless this mother conceive us in her womb, give us birth, nourish us at her breast, and lastly, unless she keep us under her care and guidance until, putting off mortal flesh, we become like the angels [Matt. 22:30]. Our weakness does not allow us to be dismissed from her school until we have been pupils all our lives. Furthermore, away from her bosom one cannot hope for any forgiveness of sins or any salvation, as Isaiah and Joel testify [Isa. 37:32; Joel 2:32]. . . . God's fatherly favour and the especial witness of spiritual life are limited to his flock, so that it is always disastrous to leave the church. . . . Wherever we see the Word of God purely preached and heard, and the sacraments administered according to Christ's institution, there, it is not to be doubted, a church of God exists. For his promise cannot fail: "Wherever two or three are gathered in my name, there I am in the midst of them" [Matt. 18:20]. . . . If [a local church] has the ministry of the Word and honours it, if it has the administration of the sacraments, it deserves without doubt to be held and considered a church. For it is certain that such things are not without fruit. In this way we preserve for the universal

church its unity, which devilish spirits have always tried to sunder; and we do not defraud of their authority those lawful assemblies which have been set up in accordance with local needs. . . .

It is also no common praise to say that Christ has chosen and set apart the church as his bride, "without spot or wrinkle" [Eph. 5:27], "his body and . . . fullness" [Eph. 1:23]. From this it follows that separation from the church is the denial of God and Christ. Hence, we must even more avoid so wicked a separation. For when with all our might we are attempting the overthrow of God's truth, we deserve to have him hurl the whole thunderbolt of his wrath to crush us. Nor can any more atrocious crime be conceived than for us by sacrilegious disloyalty to violate the marriage that the only-begotten Son of God deigned to contract with us.[3]

4

HOW TO ENJOY GOD'S LOVE

The Reforming Joy of Adoption (Galatians 4)

On the wall of my study hangs a picture of a Madonna and child. As is so often the case with such compositions, Mary looks somewhat mournful, while the baby Jesus looks like a miniature version of a full-grown man. I have it on my wall to remind me that "the past is a foreign country."[1] When I'm studying history or reading an old document, I need to remember that I'm entering a culture that is very different from my own.

I feel that distance keenly when I look at my picture of the Madonna and child because, as an evangelical, I just don't get the adoration of Mary. There are plenty of ideas that I disagree with yet can see why people find them attractive. But why the obsession with Mary?

I've nothing against her, of course. I think she's an admirable example of submission to God's will. For a young girl to be told she was pregnant through the Holy Spirit must have been alarming at all sorts of levels. I'm sure she is presented in the Scriptures as an example of faith that we're meant to follow. But then there are many other examples of faith in the Bible story that we're to emulate (as Hebrews 11 makes clear).

Over the years various extra "doctrines" have been attached to Mary:

- Her "immaculate conception" supposedly means she didn't inherit original sin.
- Her "perpetual virginity" supposedly means she was always a virgin.
- Her "assumption" supposedly means her body was taken straight to heaven, either before or as she died.
- She is supposedly a "mediatrix" or "mediator" who can intercede for us before God.

None of these claims about Mary has any basis in the Scriptures. The fact that Jesus had brothers shows that Mary had marital sex after the birth of Jesus (Mark 3:31). And the Bible is clear that there's only one mediator between God and humanity, Jesus Christ (1 Tim. 2:5).

But the interesting question is why. Why have these doctrines emerged as they have? Why has Mary become so important?

There's a clue, I think, in another title given to Mary: "the Mother of God." In 431, the Council of Ephesus described Mary as *Theotokos*, which means "bearer of God." Originally, it was more of a statement about Jesus. It was a way of saying that even though Jesus was born as a baby, he was truly God. But gradually it became a way of saying something about Mary as well, and in Western Europe it morphed into the title "Mother of God." A 1954 papal encyclical extended this to proclaim Mary officially as "the Queen of Heaven."

But why would you feel the need to call on the "Mother of God" when you can call on God the Father? The answer is that people don't think of God as a loving Father. They may think of him as the Father of Jesus but not as their Father. Or if he is a father, he's distant, aloof, cold—the kind of father who only gets involved with his children to tell them off. Imagine a child growing up with such a father. What will she do when she grazes her knee or feels unwell? She'll go to her mom, who will be compassionate, sympathetic, understanding. If dad needs to get involved, then mom will ask him. So if you think of God the Father in this way, then it's not surprising that Mary looms large. She becomes the compassionate parent to whom we go in times of need.

In Renaissance art, Jesus is usually depicted either as a child in Mary's arms or dead in Mary's arms (the latter is known as a pietà). In both cases Mary is the one in a position to offer help. The painting *Madonna Enthroned Adoring the Sleeping Child* (1475) by the Italian artist Giovanni Bellini manages to combine both motifs at the same time. The sleeping infant is flopped across Mary's knees in the kind of pose associated with a pietà. No doubt the intention was to convey the future that awaited the child. But the effect is to make Jesus doubly impotent. Meanwhile, Mary sits on a throne as the Queen of Heaven. She is the person in the picture to whom you would turn.

So changing people's view of Mary is not just about showing that many of the doctrines associated with her have no basis in God's Word. More importantly, we need to understand what God the Father is really like. We have to learn to run to the Father, confident that he'll envelop us in his arms. And that's the work of the Holy Spirit.

It's not just Roman Catholics who need to hear this message—we all need to be reminded of the Father's love. We all have a tendency to slip back into viewing God as distant, aloof, and forbidding. And when we do that, we start to live as slaves instead of sons and daughters, as people with a harsh master rather than a loving Father. It creates a life of duty rather than joy.

Living Life in Color

Think of a before-and-after advertisement. On one side is a black-and-white photo of someone looking miserable. Then that individual goes on a diet or takes a vacation. And so on the other side is a bright, colorful photo of the same person beaming with pleasure. Perhaps your Christian life is like that, only in reverse. There was a time when you were beaming with pleasure in glorious technicolor, but now your Christian life has faded into gray.

Where does joy come from, and how does it fade away? And more to the point, how can we get it back?

That's the theme of Galatians 4, a chapter in which Paul reveals the heart of God. But it's also a chapter in which Paul's own heart is laid bare. He's worried that he has wasted his time with the Galatians (4:11). He pleads with them (4:12). They used to love him. It seems that when he first arrived in Galatia, Paul had an illness, possibly an eye complaint. Imagine someone with an ugly eye afflicted by a pus discharge. You might naturally recoil. Not the Galatians. Paul says that they welcomed him "as an angel of God, as Christ Jesus" (4:14). They were so full of joy that nothing was too much trouble. If they could have, they would have torn out their own eyes and given them to Paul (4:15). But now their excitement has gone, and Paul feels like their enemy (4:16). In 4:15, he asks, "What then has become of your blessedness?" He literally says, "Where then is your blessing?" Where has your joy gone?

Paul starts by looking at where their joy came from. He does his own before-and-after snapshot. In 3:23–25, Paul talks about "we Jews." "Before faith came" in Christ, the Jews were "held captive under the law," and "the law was [their] guardian." People like Abraham who trusted in God's promise were declared right with God. But they didn't enjoy intimacy with God and spiritual freedom. They hadn't experienced that inner transformation, pictured in circumcision, that Jesus brings through the giving of the Spirit (Mark 1:8). So Old Testament believers were saved, but they didn't enjoy all the blessings that New Testament believers enjoy.

In Galatians 4:1–2, Paul says that an underage child lives like a slave. The word "guardian" in 3:25 and 4:2 was the term used for the slave with responsibility for the children of the house. The guardian supervised the children—telling them to get up, get dressed, wash themselves, and so on. It was a kind of slavery in which the children were constantly directed and monitored. But it was designed to prepare them for the freedoms of adulthood when (hopefully) the principles behind the rules had been internalized. The children were children, but their main point of contact was with their guardian. There was little intimacy or freedom. In the same way, the law constrained Israel. But it was designed to prepare for the freedom that would come in Christ when the principles behind the law were internalized in our hearts by the Holy Spirit. That's what it felt like to be an Old Testament believer. They had wonderful promises, but many of those promises were still in the future.

Imagine the heir of a great estate. He has been promised that one day he'll be rich and powerful. But as is the habit of the English aristocracy, he is first sent away to boarding school. There he lives under a strict regimen. When he gets up, when he eats, when he studies are all controlled by his schoolteachers.

Except it's worse than that. In 4:3, Paul says that the Jews "were enslaved to the elementary principles of the world." He uses the same word in 4:8 to describe how the Gentile converts used to be "enslaved to those that by nature are not gods." In the case of the Jews, Satan took God's good law and persuaded them to see it as a means of proud, God-defying self-righteousness. John Stott says,

> God intended the law to reveal sin and to drive men to Christ; Satan uses it to reveal sin and to drive men to despair. God meant the law as an interim step to man's justification; Satan uses it as the final step to his condemnation. God meant the law to be a stepping-stone to liberty; Satan uses it as a cul-de-sac.[2]

In the case of the Gentiles, we create our own gods. In the past, people worshiped nature deities or the stars and sacrificed animals to appease them. Today we live for approval, pleasure, security, or fame, and we make sacrifices to secure their blessing. Either way, the result is slavery and futility. That's the essence of all religion: work hard, be good, make sacrifices, and you might win your god's approval. And as we've seen, it doesn't work. It can't work. The result is misery.

Imagine again our child sent away to boarding school—except now we have to imagine that his teachers are cruel bullies. Not only is he enslaved by his school regimen, he's also mistreated. His life is full of fear and despair. That's what life was like for the Jews *before* Christ. That's what life is like for us all *without* Christ. We're desperately trying to make it on our own, and if we're honest, we know we're failing.

Then 4:4 begins with "But." Everything changes with the coming of Jesus. Paul says Jesus was "born under law, to redeem those who were under the law." The law shows us that we're not good enough for God, so it condemns us. It's the number-one witness for the prosecution. Jesus, the Righteous One, however, kept the law. Then he died, bearing the curse of the law (3:13). In other words, he died the death of someone condemned by the law, a death he didn't deserve but which he died in our place, "the righteous for the unrighteous, that he might bring us to God" (1 Pet. 3:18). And so he redeemed us. The law now has no power over us because the penalty it demands has been paid in full. So we're acquitted, or justified.

This truth leads to joy! No more fear, no more guilt, no more slavery.

God Sent His Son So That We Might Be Sons

But God is not done yet: "God sent forth his Son . . . so that we might receive adoption as sons" (Gal. 4:4–5). Jesus came to make us God's children with God as our Father. If you entrust yourself to Christ, then you are *in* Christ. And "in Christ Jesus you are all sons of God" (3:26).

"God sent forth his Son." Paul could have used other words to refer to Jesus. He could have said, "God sent forth the Lord Jesus" or "God sent forth his Christ." But it's important that he says "Son." We're in the Son by faith, and therefore we experience what the Son experiences. Our experience of God becomes the *Son's* experience of God. And what is his experience of God? The love of a Father. We're loved with the same love that the Father has for his *own* Son. Calvin says, "[Christ], while he is the true Son, has of himself been given us as a brother that what he has of his own by nature may become ours by benefit of adoption."[3] What is his by nature becomes ours by adoption!

Think of the Father's love for Jesus. Jesus says, "The Father loves the Son and has given all things into his hand" (John 3:35). "The Father loves the Son and shows him all that he himself is doing" (John 5:20). Jesus prays, "Father . . . you loved me before the foundation of the world" (John 17:24). This is an eternal love that shares everything.

Or if that is too abstract to get your head around, think of it like this: Jesus says, "As the Father has loved me, so have I loved you" (John 15:9). What does the Father's love look like? It looks like the love of Jesus. Think of Jesus meeting the outcast leper and touching him. Think of Jesus seeing the crowds and being moved with compassion. Think of Jesus meeting a grieving sister and weeping alongside her. Think of Jesus healing the sick, feeding the hungry, welcoming the children. Think of him hanging on the cross, crying, "Father, forgive them." This is what the Father's love is like. We see it clearly in the love of the Son.

In Ephesians 1:4–5, Paul says that the Father's love is the beginning and end of our salvation: "In love he predestined us for adoption to himself as sons through Jesus Christ, according to the purpose of his will." "Predestined" means "planned." Jesus doesn't have to win God over or persuade him to welcome us. The whole plan of salvation starts with the Father's love. And it ends with our adoption, with us experiencing his love. And that love is channeled "through Jesus Christ." The love that flows to us flows through Jesus. God's love for us is his love for his Son.

Not only that, but also this is God's pleasure. You are his pleasure. He was pleased to save you. He is pleased to call you "my son" or "my daughter."

The secret to enjoying God is to realize that he enjoys you.

God Sent the Spirit of His Son So That We Might Know That We Are Sons

But even this was not enough, not for God. It was not enough for him to make us his children. He wants us to know that we're his children. He wants us to experience his love. And that's why he sent the Holy Spirit. Galatians 4:6 says, "And because you are sons, God has sent the Spirit of his Son into our hearts." The reason why God sent the Spirit is so that we can experience what it is to be sons and daughters loved by our Father. And notice how the Spirit is described. Most of the time in Galatians Paul simply refers to "the Spirit." Often in the New Testament he's described as "the Holy Spirit." But here Paul calls him "the Spirit of his Son." Our experience of the Spirit is the experience of the Son, for the Spirit is the Spirit of the Son. The Spirit enables us to experience what Jesus experiences.

So the Father has given us the Spirit of his Son so that we can enjoy the experience of his Son, so that we know what it is to be sons *like the Son*, so that we can enjoy the love the Son experiences from the Father.

God gave his Son up to the whip, the thorns, the nails, the darkness, and the experience of forsakenness so that you could be his child. No wonder he sends the Spirit of his Son. He doesn't want you to miss out on all that the Son has secured for you. This is his eternal plan: that you should enjoy his fatherly love.

The world is full of people searching for love and intimacy. Many sexual encounters and affairs are a desperate attempt to numb a sense of loneliness. Many people who seem to have it all feel empty inside. The actor and director Liv Ullmann once said, "Hollywood is loneliness beside the swimming pool." We were made for more. The reason why we yearn for intimacy is that we were made for intimacy: we were made to love God and be loved by him. And this is what the Father gives us by sending his Son and by sending the Spirit of his Son.

What Does This Intimacy Look Like?

We Can Talk to God Like Children Talk to Their Father

"The Spirit . . . [cries], 'Abba! Father!'" (Gal. 4:6). The Spirit gives us the confidence to address God as our Father. A number of our friends have adopted children. And it's always a special moment when the adopted child starts calling them "Mom" and "Dad." God is infinite, holy, majestic. He's a consuming fire before whom angels cover their faces. He made all things and controls all things. Can you imagine calling him "Father"? Of course you can! You do it every day when you pray—most of the time without even thinking about it. How is that possible? Step back and think about it for a moment, and you'll realize what an amazing miracle it is that any of us should call God "Father." But we do so every time we pray, through the Spirit of the Son. This is how John Calvin puts it:

> With what confidence would anyone address God as "Father"? Who would break forth into such rashness as to claim for himself the honour of a son of God unless we had been adopted as children of grace in Christ? . . . But because the narrowness of our hearts cannot comprehend God's boundless favour, not only is Christ the pledge and guarantee of our adoption, but he moves the Spirit as witness to us of the same adoption, through whom with free and full voice we may cry, "Abba, Father."[4]

Think of those adopted children saying "Mom" and "Dad" for the first time. What must that feel like for them? Perhaps they do so tentatively at first. They're still feeling their way in the relationship. And that's often what it's like for new Christians, feeling their way in this new relationship. But think, too, what it means for the parents. It's a joyful moment. It's a sign that their children are beginning to feel like children. It's a moment of pleasure. And so it is for God every time you call him "Father." Remember, he planned our adoption "in accordance with his pleasure" (Eph. 1:5 NIV).

We Can Think of God Like Children Think of Their Father

"So you are no longer a slave, but a son" (Gal. 4:7). Slaves are always worried about doing what they're told or doing the right thing. They fear the disapproval of their master because there's always the possibility that they might be punished or sacked. Children never have to fear being sacked. They may sometimes be disciplined, but as with any good parent, it's always for their good. God is the best of parents. And we never have to fear being sacked. You can't stop being a child of God—you're not fostered. You're adopted for life, and life for you is eternal!

The cry "Abba! Father!" is not just for moments of intimacy. It was actually the cry that a child shouted when in need. One of the joys of my life is that I'm good friends with lots of children. Charis always cries out, "Tim!" when she sees me. Tayden wants me to read his *Where's Wally?* book with him. Again. Tyler wants me to throw him over my shoulder and swing him around. Josie wants to tell me everything in her head all at once in her lisping voice. They all enjoy having me around. But here's what I've noticed. Whenever any of them falls over or gets knocked, my parental instinct kicks in, and I rush to help. But it's not me they want in those moments. They run past me looking for Mom or Dad. They cry out, "Dad!" and Tim won't do. That's what

"Abba! Father!" means. When we're in need, we cry out to God because the Spirit assures us that God is our Father and that our Father cares about what's happening to his children.

We Can Depend on God Like Children Depend on Their Father

"And if [you are] a son, then [you are] an heir through God" (Gal. 4:7). When Paul talks about "sonship," he's not being sexist. Quite the opposite. In the Roman world only male children could inherit. So when Paul says "we" ("male and female," 3:28) are "sons," he's saying that in God's family, men *and women* inherit. Everyone is included. And what we inherit is God's glorious new world. But more than that, we inherit God himself. In all the uncertainties of this life, we can depend on him. He will lead us home, and our home is his glory.

What could be better than sharing in the infinite love and infinite joy of the eternal Father with the eternal Son? Think of what you might aspire to in life—your greatest hopes and dreams. And then multiply them by a hundred. Think of winning Olympic gold or lifting the World Cup. Think of being a billionaire and owning a Caribbean island. Think of your love life playing out like the most heartwarming romantic movie. Good. But not as good as enjoying God.

Or let's do it in reverse. Think of your worst fears and nightmares: losing a loved one, never finding someone to marry, losing your health, not having children. Bad! But Paul says, "I consider that the sufferings of this present time are not worth comparing with the glory that is to be revealed to us" (Rom. 8:18). The only time Jesus is quoted as saying, "Abba, Father," is in the Garden of Gethsemane as he sweats blood at the prospect of the cross (Mark 14:36). Even when you feel crushed by your pain, God is still your Abba, Father.

Where does joy come from? It comes from being children of God. How can we enjoy God? By living as his children. How can we please God? By believing he loves us as he loves his Son.

Rediscovered Joy

This was the joy the Galatians had experienced. This is why they welcomed Paul as if he were Christ Jesus himself (Gal. 4:14). But now, as we know, this joy is gone. Why? What have they traded it for?

> Formerly, when you did not know God, you were enslaved to those that by nature are not gods. But now that you have come to know God, or rather to be known by God, how can you turn back again to the weak and worthless elementary principles of the world, whose slaves you want to be once more? You observe days and months and seasons and years! (4:8–10)

The Galatians used to be pagans. They used to worship idols, "those that by nature are not gods." Now they're turning to the law of Moses, to the observance of circumcision and special days. They think that's an advance: from paganism to faith to law. But the big irony is this: Paul says it's actually a return to paganism. That's because they're turning to the satanic misuse of the law—not the law as the promise of a coming righteousness in Christ but the law as a means of *self*-righteousness. And that's paganism. The essence of paganism is that we appease our god's wrath because we offer sacrifices. The essence of the gospel is that God *himself* appeases his wrath because he offers his Son as the sacrifice to end all sacrifices. The essence of paganism is that we do everything we can to earn the approval of our god. The essence of the gospel is that God does everything we can't to *give* his approval to his people.

But the point of Galatians 4 is that Christians all too easily slip back into this pagan way of thinking. We think we need to earn God's approval and turn to some kind of law to do this. If you're living your life in black and white, then the chances are that this is why.

No wonder Paul is perplexed (4:20). God sent his Son, and God sent the Spirit of his Son. And you think that's not enough? You think you need to win his approval? Paul says that these spiritual forces are "weak and worthless" (4:9)—literally, "weak and destitute." They have neither the power nor the resources to make you happy.

And all the time the Father's arms are open wide, ready to scoop us up into his embrace.

Living as a Slave or Living as a Child

Have a look at the description of living as a slave and living as a child of God in table 4.1. Which best describes you?

When you find yourself in the *living as a slave* column, what do you do next? Try harder? Of course not—that's the reaction of a slave!

You turn in repentance to God. You say, "Heavenly Father, I'm sorry that I sometimes live like a slave. Help me to live like a child. Help me to trust in your fatherly love and care. May the Spirit of your Son help me to feel what it's like to be loved like your Son." Look to the cross. That's where we see God's love writ large. That's where we see God's commitment to making us children (see table 4.1).

Living as a Slave	Living as a Child
Having (or missing) a daily time of Bible reading and prayer feels like a burden.	Reading the Bible and praying each day feels like talking to your Father.
You're anxious about money, grades, or family.	You're concerned about money, grades, or family, but you're happy to trust your Father.
Success and failure have a big impact on your mood.	You see success and failure in the bigger perspective of being a child of God.
You often try to second-guess what others are thinking so that you can please them.	The views of other people matter, but the view of your Father matters more.
You have to fix problems.	You can live with uncertainty because your Father is in control.
You feel the need to perform to be accepted.	You feel accepted by your Father even when you've sinned.
You're risk averse because you fear failure.	You don't fear failure because you already see yourself as a failure-turned-child.
When service feels like a duty, you knuckle down.	When service feels like a duty, you remind yourself of your Father's love.
You're defensive when criticized.	You're open to criticism because your identity as a child of God is secure.
You worry about the future.	You think, "In the worst-case scenario, I'm still a child of God and an heir of glory."
You'll do anything to avoid disappointing people.	You're not controlled by what people think because you have the approval of your Father.
You feel guilty if you have to miss a prayer meeting.	You feel disappointed if you have to miss a prayer meeting.

Table 4.1

Reflection Questions

How might we apply our identity as God's children to each of these situations?

1. Pete is a great contributor to church life. He's on every rotation, and he takes the initiative to care for others. But lately he's been getting short tempered. "Why don't other people pull their weight?" he asks.
2. Last week Suzie suddenly walked out of your meeting. It turns out that people were talking about why they don't observe Halloween, and Suzie took offense because she lets her children go trick-or-treating. She feels judged by everyone.
3. Paula used to be a bubbly young woman, but lately she has become withdrawn and quiet. Then you discover that she's struggling with anorexia. "I just want to be beautiful," she tells you.
4. Jack wants to talk to you about his giving. But as you chat, it becomes clear that what he's really worried about is his spending. He finds it difficult not to buy things on a whim when he's out shopping.

Getting Personal

1. How do you view God?
2. How do you assume God views you?
3. How does your adoption as God's child shape or reshape these assumptions?
4. Review table 4.1 above. In what ways are you living as a child of God? In what ways are you living as a slave? What are you going to do next?

Voices of the Reformation: Our Father

This extract is taken from the beginning of Calvin's explanation of the Lord's Prayer in his *Institutes*. When Calvin says, "We cannot seek help anywhere else," or speaks of not looking to the "pleas of others," he has in mind prayers directed to Mary and other saints. Calvin says that to go to God via Mary is to accuse him of being so cruel that he needs her to win him over. In reality, God's love is "boundless." Even if you personally do not pray to Mary, think of how often you look to yourself or others rather than turning to your heavenly Father in prayer.

> First, at the very threshold . . . we ought to offer all prayer to God only in Christ's name, as it cannot be agreeable to him in any other name. For in calling God "Father," we put forward the name "Christ." With what confidence would anyone address God as "Father"? Who would break forth into such rashness as to claim for himself the honour of a son of God unless we had been adopted as children of grace in Christ? He, while he is the true Son, has of himself been given us as a brother that what he has of his own by nature may become ours by benefit of adoption if we embrace this great blessing with sure faith. Accordingly, John says that power has been given to those who believe in the name of the only-begotten Son of God, that they too may become children of God [John 1:12].
>
> Therefore God both calls himself our Father and would have us so address him. By the great sweetness of this name he frees us from all distrust, since no greater feeling of love can be found elsewhere than in the Father. Therefore he could not attest his own boundless love toward us with any surer proof than the fact that we are called "children of God" [1 John 3:1]. But just as he surpasses all men in goodness and mercy, so is his love greater and more excellent than all our parents' love. Hence, though all earthly fathers should divest themselves of all feeling of fatherhood and forsake

their children, he will never fail us [Ps. 27:10; Isa. 63:16], since he cannot deny himself [2 Tim. 2:13]. For we have this promise: "If you, although you are evil, know how to give good gifts to your children, how much more will your Father, who is in heaven" [Matt. 7:11]? Similarly, in the prophet: "Can a woman forget her . . . children? . . . Even if she forgets, yet I shall not forget you" [Isa. 49:15]. But a son cannot give himself over to the safekeeping of a stranger and an alien without at the same time complaining either of his father's cruelty or want. Thus, if we are his sons, we cannot seek help anywhere else than from him without reproaching him for poverty, or want of means, or cruelty and excessive rigour. . . .

But because the narrowness of our hearts cannot comprehend God's boundless favour, not only is Christ the pledge and guarantee of our adoption, but he moves the Spirit as witness to us of the same adoption, through whom with free and full voice we may cry, "Abba, Father" [Gal. 4:6; Rom. 8:15]. Therefore, whenever any hesitation shall hinder us, let us remember to ask him to correct our fearfulness, and to set before us that Spirit that he may guide us to pray boldly.[5]

5

HOW TO DO GOD'S WILL

The Reforming Joy of Life in the Spirit (Galatians 5)

By this point, you may be thinking that sooner or later the link between Galatians and the Reformation is going to become somewhat strained. After all, we've covered the big themes of the authority of Scripture and justification by faith. But in fact we're about to get to the heart of the issues. You don't have to take my word for it. We can listen in to Luther himself in conversation with Erasmus.

Desiderius Erasmus was Europe's leading celebrity academic. In 1524, he published an attack on Luther titled *The Freedom of the Will*. Erasmus argued that human beings have the capacity to please God. We have the power to choose good, he argued. God's grace helps us choose, but the choice is ours. And while we may not be able to repay the debt we owe to God, Erasmus said that God is prepared to accept our limited good works as worthy of merit.

This, says Luther, goes right to the heart of the issue. At the end of his response to Erasmus, *The Bondage of the Will*, Luther says,

> My dear Erasmus . . . I praise and commend you highly for this also, that unlike all the rest you alone have attacked the real issue, the essence of the matter in dispute, and have not wearied me with irrelevancies about the papacy, purgatory, indulgences, and such like trifles (for trifles they are rather than basic issues), with which almost everyone hitherto has gone hunting for me without success. You and you alone have seen the question on which everything hinges, and have aimed at the vital spot.[1]

In other words, this is the core issue at stake in the Reformation: Do we have the capacity in ourselves to choose good? Can we please God? Erasmus said yes. And God lets us squeeze into heaven if we choose him and do good works. Luther said no. Or at least not until God himself changes us by his Spirit. Left to ourselves, we are utterly helpless and hopeless.

How to Be Good

The problem according to Luther is not that we're compelled to do wrong by some external force. When he talks about "the bondage of the will," he doesn't mean that someone or something is making us do what we don't want to do. What holds us in bondage is *us*! Our sinful and selfish desires rule our wills. We can do only what we want to do, and we only want to do what is contrary to God's will. Ever since Adam, our hearts have had a deep-seated bias against God.

As far as Erasmus was concerned, we just need to try harder. But Luther realized our problem was much more fundamental than that. Our problem is not that we're lazy or ignorant (as Erasmus thought) but that we're sinners deep down to the very core of our being. Indeed, working harder kind of makes things worse. Our renewed efforts might produce actions that are *outwardly* righteous (more prayer, more charitable donations). But inwardly our hearts are even more proud and independent. It's like wallpapering a house whose foundations are collapsing.

Instead, Luther realized that if we're ever going to love or please God, we need a radical inner transformation. And that's what the Holy Spirit does. The Old Testament prophets described this as a "circumcision of the heart." The outward sign of circumcision was a promise of the inner work of the Spirit changing our hearts (Rom. 2:28–29). John the Baptist said of Jesus, "I have baptized you with water, but he will baptize you with the Holy Spirit" (Mark 1:8). Jesus himself calls it being "born again"—that's how radical it is (John 3:3–6). We have to begin all over again as new people.

When we choose to reject Christ, we make a real choice. There are two options before us, and no one is forcing us to choose against our will. The problem is that our will is so set against God that we will not and cannot choose Christ. You can offer children a choice between sprouts and chocolate. It's a real choice with both on the table in front of them. But a typical child is going to choose chocolate every time. In a similar way, but with much more inevitability, we're presented with a choice. On the one hand, we see the pleasures of sin and living life as we choose. On the other hand, we see a pathetic figure hanging on a cross and the constraints of living under God's restrictive rule. And every time, we choose sin instead of Christ.

Our hearts are hardwired to reject God. We're like the needle of a compass floating freely. It's free to point in any direction, but it always points toward magnetic north. Likewise, we're free to go in any direction, but we always point away from God and toward sin.

But then the Holy Spirit opens our eyes. Instead of the pleasures of sin, we see hatred, pain, and death. Instead of God's rule seeming restrictive, we see him as a loving Father. And instead of a pathetic figure on the cross, we see our King, full of love, dying in our place to rescue us from our guilt. We see Jesus, the Morning Star of heaven, the perfect Image of God, the true Man, the kind Husband, the faithful Friend. We see that following him leads to forgiveness, freedom, life, and the promise of eternal glory. Our blind eyes are opened. Our deaf ears are cleared. Our dead hearts are renewed. And now we choose Christ—of course we do. But the "of course" is all down to the Spirit.

As we saw earlier, the central message of Galatians is that righteousness comes through faith in Christ. But this saving faith comes "through the Spirit." Galatians 5:5 says, "For *through the Spirit*, by faith, we ourselves eagerly wait for the hope of righteousness." Yes, we're saved by faith in Christ. But that faith is itself a gift from God (Eph. 2:8–9). Without the rebirth of the Spirit, we would never choose to put our faith in Christ.

But not only does the Spirit cause our faith, he is also the result of our faith. He is given in response to faith to help us continue to live for Christ. So the Spirit acts on our hearts to enable us to become Christians, and then the Spirit comes to indwell our hearts so we go on living as Christians. The order is something like what is shown in figure 5.1:

We're born again by the Spirit.

↓

We put our faith in Christ.

↓

We're justified and adopted.

↓

The Spirit comes to live within us.

↓

We realize that we're God's children, and the
Spirit gives us the power and desire to do good.

Figure 5.1

In the first half of Galatians the focus is on faith in Christ. But in the second half the language of "faith" is replaced by the language of the "Spirit." The words "faith" and "believe" occur nineteen times in chapters 1–3 but only twice in chapters 4–6. Meanwhile, the word "Spirit" occurs four times in chapters 1–3 and eleven times in chapters 4–6. How do we live a life that pleases God? Not by going back to the law of Moses but through life in the Spirit.

Erasmus clearly thought that people already had enough power in themselves to do good. He defined free choice as "a power of the human will by which a man can apply himself to the things which lead to eternal salvation, or turn away from them."[2] Luther replied, "You do not realize how much you attribute to it by this pronoun 'itself'—its very own self!—when you say it can 'apply itself'; for this means that you completely exclude the Holy Spirit with all his power, as superfluous and unnecessary."[3] Luther's point, and Paul's point, is that we need the Holy Spirit in order to choose good and do good.

Luther's opponents accused the Reformation of undermining good works and social order. If people thought they were saved by faith alone without works, then they would feel free to do whatever they wanted. Erasmus said, "Lutherans seek only two things—wealth and wives. . . . To them the gospel means the right to live as they please."[4] The result would surely be anarchy.

Luther turned this argument on its head. His famous "Ninety-Five Theses" were not his first stab at provoking a debate. A few weeks earlier he had posted the "Ninety-Seven Theses" (though it may have been "Ninety-Nine"). They included an attack on the Greek philosopher Aristotle, who had made something of a comeback in the medieval period. As it happens, no one took much notice of Luther's "Ninety-Seven Theses." Yet they were much more central to the driving thought of the Reformation. So when Luther was summoned to account for his actions before his Augustinian order, it was to the themes in the "Ninety-Seven" that he returned. Aristotle said we become righteous by doing right acts. Your identity is the result of your actions, what you *achieve*. Luther said that this gets things completely the wrong way around. In the gospel our identity is a gift from God, something you *receive*. God makes us his children, and then our actions flow from our new identity. Unbelievers can be constrained by laws and peer pressure. But a life of wholehearted righteous living is possible only if God makes us new people.

Slavery Disguised as Freedom

What Erasmus and Luther had in common was a concern that people should obey God—even though they fundamentally disagreed on how this happened. But today few people are interested in obeying God. Indeed, today being "good" is seen as being true to yourself. Personal freedom is the "good" that trumps everything else in our culture. "If I want to get drunk, then I'll get drunk. If I want to lose my temper, then I'll lose my temper. If I want to watch porn, then I'll watch porn. That's real freedom." Faith and law are not the only choices. There's a third option: license, living as we please.

But Paul says, "Only do not use your freedom as an opportunity for the flesh, but through love serve one another" (Gal. 5:13). Here's a restriction and a command. So is this *law by another name*? Have we just unearthed the unwelcome small print? How can serving others be freedom?

We need to take a step back and think about the nature of freedom. Our culture defines freedom as having a multiplicity of choices. We're free because we choose between different candidates at an election or different brands of cornflakes in our supermarket.

But think about what it means for God to be free. God is able to do what he wants, but he's not free to sin. So ultimate freedom is not *having the choice to sin*. Instead of being about having a multiplicity of choices, true freedom is *the ability to enjoy the best or be what you're meant to be*. Otherwise, God is not as free as I am. I can choose to sin or not to sin. God cannot choose to do so. But God is more free than I am. He has the ability always to choose the best.

Or think of it like this: Will we have a vote in heaven? No, we won't need to vote out bad rulers in the hope of a better ruler because we will have the *best* ruler of all, God himself. So ultimate freedom is not *having a choice or a vote*; rather, it's *the ability to enjoy the best*.

So what does it mean for a Christian to be free? It's the ability to enjoy the best, and that means enjoying God. Freedom is defined by joy, true joy. Indulging your selfish desires is a very superficial form of freedom. It's like a teenager saying, "My parents have given me the freedom to go wherever I want, and

I'm going to use my new freedom to walk across the highway." It's like a released prisoner saying, "I'm going to use my new freedom to live in a cell." It's like a restored alcoholic saying, "I'm going to use my new freedom to get drunk all the time." Your actions are not free if they're enslaving you!

So freedom, goodness, and joy are not in tension. They're different aspects of the same thing. Freedom is the ability to enjoy and be the best.

The prudish, dour life of legalism and the wild excesses of license look like polar opposites. But Paul says they have more in common than you might at first think. They're both ways of living according to the flesh.

License indulges the sinful desires of the flesh. "Do not use your freedom as an opportunity for the flesh," says Paul in 5:13. License is an attempt by the flesh to *replace God as Lord*. Instead, we live how we choose.

But law is also a way of living according to the flesh. In 3:2–3, Paul equates "the works of the law" with an attempt to be "perfected by the flesh." Law is living by the flesh because law *replaces God as Savior*. It's an attempt to be righteous through our own abilities and efforts. The result is conceit if we do well and envy if we don't (5:26).

Life in the Spirit

The alternative to law and license is life in the Spirit. John Stott says,

> It is no good giving me a play like Hamlet or King Lear, and telling me to write a play like that. Shakespeare could do it; I can't. And it is no good showing me a life like the life of Jesus and telling me to live a life like that. Jesus could do it; I can't. But if the genius of Shakespeare could come

> and live in me, then I could write plays like his. And if the Spirit of Jesus could come and live in me, then I could live a life like His.[5]

That's what happens when we become Christians. The Spirit of Jesus lives in us and we start to become like Jesus. We're set free to choose the best, and the best is Jesus. This is how Paul puts it in Galatians 5:16–17:

> But I say, walk by the Spirit, and you will not gratify the desires of the flesh. For the desires of the flesh are against the Spirit, and the desires of the Spirit are against the flesh, for these are opposed to each other, to keep you from doing the things you want to do.

At first sight this sounds more like struggle than freedom. The point is this: before the Spirit came into our lives, we were slaves to sin and idolatry (4:8). But now the Spirit gives us new desires: a desire for God and a desire for holiness. So now there's a choice. We can be anxious, or we can trust God. We can fear others, or we can fear God. We can get angry, or we can find our vindication with God. Because there's a choice, we experience this new freedom as conflict. Indeed, we never quite get to do what we want. Galatians 5:17 says that the flesh and the Spirit "are opposed to each other, to keep you from doing the things you want to do." When we do good things, our sinful desires are disappointed. When we do bad things, our new Spirit-inspired desires are disappointed.

Like the Spirit's role in testifying that God is our Father, it's extraordinary how life in the Spirit feels so ordinary. Christians feel their lack of change acutely. But this is the result of the Spirit's work. And it's a dramatic, miraculous work. The irony is that we often feel it as failure! We feel our failure to be the people we want to be. But those very ordinary feelings are themselves an extraordinary work of the Spirit. They reflect our Spirit-given longing for God.

We want to know what to do to become more like Jesus. And yes, there are things we can and should do. But we're not the primary agent of change in our lives. The virtues listed in 5:22–23 are "the fruit of the Spirit." You can't command a tree to grow fruit. It grows fruit because it is alive. And you can't command someone to be loving, joyful, peaceful, and so on. That fruit is produced because the Spirit is giving us spiritual life. This is so encouraging. There's a relentless inevitability about the Spirit's work. Yes, it's a lifetime process, and yes, sometimes it can feel to us like it's going in reverse. But the Spirit will sanctify us.

Love Is the Catalyst of Change

The Spirit doesn't just zap new desires into our hearts. His work of changing us is closely connected with his work of testifying that we're God's children—the role Paul described in Galatians 4:6–7. Our bias against God is reversed as we realize that God is for us. Instead of drawing *away* from him *in fear*, we're drawn *to* him *in love*. Love is key, the catalyst of change. The more we recognize God's fatherly love for us, the more we love him in return. The more we recognize God's goodness, the more we want to be good. The more we recognize our identity as God's children, the more we're free to serve others in love. As children of God, we don't need to prove ourselves, worry what others think, or be anxious about tomorrow. As heirs of God, we don't need to secure our future, get angry when things go wrong, or chase the treasures of this world.

We Live by Following the Leading of the Spirit

In the case of our justification, we did nothing, and Christ did everything. Even our faith was the Spirit's work. But with our sanctification we have a role to play. *Our* job is to live by the Spirit (Gal. 5:16), to be led by the Spirit (5:18), to keep in step with the Spirit (5:25).

Think of swimming in a river. The current of the Spirit's work is carrying us downstream toward holiness. What are you going to do? You could swim upstream, against the flow, in the wrong direction. Or you could swim downstream with the Spirit's energy, led in the right direction toward Jesus.

In 5:18, the phrase "led by the Spirit" is the language of shepherding. A few years ago I visited Iraq and saw shepherds on the hillsides with flocks of sheep following behind them. First-century shepherds were the same. They didn't herd their flocks with sheepdogs. They led them because the sheep trusted them. The flesh tells us that temptation offers better pasture. But the flesh can't be trusted. The flesh says that sexual indulgence is pleasure without harm. The flesh says that anger is justified. The flesh says that you need to prove yourself. But 5:21 says that the flesh is leading us to destruction. Meanwhile, the Spirit is leading us toward green pastures. Our job is to trust his lead.

In 5:25, the image is of the Spirit as a trailblazer. Imagine walking through a thick jungle. The Spirit goes ahead forming a path. Our job is to follow in his footsteps along the trail he's creating. If we step to the side, then we'll go off course and become enmeshed in the jungle.

That doesn't mean that life is smooth or holiness is easy. It's a struggle, as Paul makes clear in 5:16–17. But without the Spirit, *there wouldn't even be a struggle*. We used to be a dead corpse eaten away by sin, or a trussed-up body entirely under sin's power. Or rather, we used to actively collude in our own destruction. We were being dragged off to hell without a fight because it was the direction in which we wanted to go. But the Spirit has opened our eyes to the horror of sin and the beauty of God. Now we're pulled in two directions. Our job is to go with the grain of the Spirit's work, flow with the current of the Spirit's energy, walk in line with the Spirit's lead.

The Leading of the Spirit Is Obvious

How do we distinguish between the pull of the flesh and the leading of the Spirit? We can often imagine that this is some kind of mystical or mysterious process. As a result, Paul's teaching feels beyond our experience—something for super-Christians.

But Galatians 5:19 says that it's *obvious*: "The acts of the flesh are obvious" (NIV). While sometimes we have to make complex ethical choices, that's not Paul's focus here. Most of the time in our day-to-day life, we know what's wrong and what's right. You don't need a Bible study or theological consultation to tell you that sexual immorality, impurity and debauchery, idolatry and witchcraft, and so on are wrong (5:19–21).

On the positive side, Paul lists the fruit of the Spirit and says, "Against such things there is no law" (5:23). The false teachers said people needed the law of Moses. But Paul says you don't need a set of rules to tell you to show "love, joy, peace, patience, kindness, goodness, faithfulness, gentleness, self-control." Indeed, the Spirit produces a life that's superior to law. You can't have a commandment like "Thou shalt not lack joy." You can't legislate love, joy, peace, and so on. But the Spirit creates a life no law can express. Paul is echoing the Sermon on the Mount, where Jesus takes the Ten Commandments and makes them a matter of the heart (Matt. 5:21–48).

So you don't have to wait for a "word" or a sense of peace. Paul's not talking here about guidance for specific decisions. He's saying, "You have an impulse in you to do wrong—that's the flesh. And you have an impulse in you to do right—that's the Spirit. Follow the impulse of the Spirit." It's not a mystery. It's "obvious." Every inclination in you to do good, to please God, to enjoy God, to pray, to serve, to love—that's the leading of the Spirit. Follow it.

We Live by Dying Every Day

Galatians 5:24 says, "And those who belong to Christ Jesus have crucified the flesh with its passions and desires." There's no room here for compromise. We're to oppose the murderous intent of the flesh with murderous intent. This is a do-or-die battle to the death. The flesh is trying to kill us, so we kill the flesh. Paul is echoing Jesus's call to cut off our hand or pluck out our eye if it causes us to sin (Mark 9:43–48). We're to avoid temptation at all costs and say a decisive *no* when it first arises. The Reformers called this "mortification." Today that term is used to describe social embarrassment ("I was mortified when I dropped the tray of drinks"). But Calvin used it to mean killing sin in our lives.[6]

In Galatians 2:20, Paul said, "I have been crucified with Christ. It is no longer I who live, but Christ who lives in me." Here the Christian is passive, and Christ is active. Our old self dies with Christ, and we rise to a new life. This is the foundation of our sanctification. Jesus has broken the power of sin. That's why Paul uses the metaphor of crucifixion. It ties our violent opposition to sin back to the cross. In Galatians 5, though, we're the ones who are active. On the basis of Christ's victory, we enter the battle. Verse 24 is in the past tense: Christians "have crucified the flesh." That's what happens when we first turn to

Christ in repentance. Repentance is a decisive break with sin as we turn back to God. But that doesn't mean the job is done. In this life we never move on from repentance. This decisive past act now determines the pattern of our lives.

Imagine hearing Winston Churchill say in 1944, "We declared war on Germany in 1939, and Germany continues to fight against us." The implication would be clear: we must fight on. In the same way Paul is saying, "You crucified the flesh when you first became a Christian, and that act continues to define your attitude to the flesh." You've declared war on the flesh. So fight. No one has called a cease-fire—certainly not the flesh. It's still hell-bent on your destruction.

The first thesis of Luther's famous "Ninety-Five Theses" is this: "When our Lord and Master, Jesus Christ, said, 'Repent,' He called for the entire life of believers to be one of penitence."[7] Luther adds that "penitence" refers not to a sacrament administered by the clergy (thesis 2) but to the daily "mortification" of the flesh (thesis 3). In other words, repentance is not simply what you do when you first become a Christian; it's also how you continue to live and grow as a Christian. As Paul has emphasized all the way through Galatians, we continue as Christians in the same way we started as Christians, through faith and repentance.

A life of mortifying the flesh or continual repentance means

- saying no whenever you're tempted and
- saying sorry whenever you sin.

You might want to think of repenting of sin in two ways:

- *Day by day*: reviewing your actions over the previous twenty-four hours so that you can repudiate your sin and ask God for forgiveness

- *Sin by sin*: whenever you're conscious of having sinned, repenting before God in the moment and, if other people are involved, saying sorry to them

The word translated "desires" in 5:16–17 is literally "*over*desires." The desires of the flesh are sometimes desires for bad things. But more often they're desires for good things that have grown too big. They matter more to us than God because we think they'll deliver more for us than God. We *over*desire them. In other words, they've become idols.

It's good to desire to be married, for example, but if our unfulfilled desire for marriage makes us bitter, then it has become an idolatrous overdesire. It's good to be in control, but if our desire for control makes us manipulative, then it has become an idolatrous overdesire. It's good to desire the approval of your peers, but if our desire for approval leads us into sin, then it has become an idolatrous overdesire. In effect, our desire for marriage, control, or approval has become more important to us than God. Instead of finding joy in God, we're looking for it elsewhere. The indication that this is what's happening is sinful acts or sinful attitudes.

This means that sometimes we need to look behind our sins to see their underlying idolatrous overdesires. If you're a gardener, then you'll know that it's no use cutting down weeds. To get rid of them, you need to dig out the roots. In the same way, we need to repent not just of our sinful acts but also of our underlying idolatrous overdesires. We need to attack the very roots of our sin.[8]

By Dying We Truly Live

You may be thinking, "All this talk of dying to sin doesn't sound like much fun. Where's the joy in self-denial?" But here's where things get surprising. In his influential book, *New Rules: Searching for Self-Fulfillment in a World Turned Upside Down*,[9] Daniel Yankelovich charts the development of what he describes as a new ethic—"the duty to self ethic"—which is replacing the old ethic of self-denial, duty to others, and deferred gratification. Daniel Yankelovich's instinct was that the move to self-fulfillment would be liberating. But he admits that the evidence shows the opposite. After three thousand in-depth interviews and many more questionnaires, he concedes that the search for self-fulfillment has been futile. If life is about self-fulfillment, then it's only as good as your last experience. If it's about self-expression, then it's only as good as your last performance. It's all precarious, and we're all insecure. So our generation suffers far more from depression, anxiety, and mental disorders. David Wells explains,

> Whereas the older kind of success was durable, this is not. This is fleeting. It is dependent not on its own quality but on the perceptions of others. Perceptions, however, are fickle, changing, quickly superseded, quickly forgotten. Success today, therefore, has to be constantly renewed.[10]

Think of the Christians you know who are most preoccupied with themselves, their desires, their status. And then think of the Christians you know who are most preoccupied with serving others and God's glory. Which are the happier?

Jesus said, "If anyone would come after me, let him deny himself and take up his cross and follow me. For whoever would save his life will lose it, but whoever loses his life for my sake and the gospel's will save it" (Mark 8:34–35). Ultimately, this is about living for the glories of the new creation (as Mark 8:38 makes clear). But it begins now. Those who live for themselves are relationally and emotionally impoverished. Those who live for Christ and for others are rich beyond wealth.

Our relentless desire for quick pleasures is like a diet of whipped cream and sugar icing. Everyone enjoys a little bit of cream. But if that's all you ever eat, then you'll quickly get ill. That's our culture. We've overdosed on self-fulfillment, and now we feel sick. But virtue is deeply nourishing for the soul. It creates lasting contentment and joy. Yes, following Christ does mean suffering and sacrifice. But we're also becoming truly human. We're becoming people who know God and feel his pleasure. We're living life as it is meant to be lived, rediscovering true and lasting joy.

An Invitation

The false teachers in Galatia were like people trying to pull a balloon into the shape of a box. At best, you get a pathetic imitation of a balloon. At worst, you tear it.

The false teachers said the "shape" of a Christian was a law-abiding Jew. But the shape of a Christian is Christ (Gal. 4:19) or love (5:6, 14).

And the false teachers said we pull ourselves into shape. But that's more likely to tear people apart. Instead, we change through faith in Christ and the life of the Spirit. The nouns "Spirit" and "breath" are the same word in Greek. God breathes his Spirit, or breath, into us so that we take on the shape of Christ.

"For freedom Christ has set us free; stand firm therefore, and do not submit again to a yoke of slavery" (5:1). Both Galatians and the Reformation are an invitation to freedom—the freedom to enjoy God and be who you were meant to be. This is real joy, a joy worth finding.

Reflection Questions

1. What difference does it make knowing that the Spirit is the primary agent of change in our lives?
2. What's the link between the sanctifying work of the Spirit and the Spirit's work of testifying that we're God's children?
3. What does it look like in practice for you to follow the lead of the Spirit?
4. What does it look like for you to crucify the flesh?

Getting Personal

Galatians 5 describes three ways to live (see table 5.1).

Law (Gal. 5:1–12)	License (Gal. 5:13–15)	Life in the Spirit (Gal. 5:16–25)
I am ruled by a law.	I am ruled by selfish desires.	I am ruled by the Spirit.
I obey because I feel I ought to even though I don't want to.	I don't obey, because I don't want to.	I obey because I want to, for the Spirit gives me new desires.
I replace Christ as my Savior.	I replace Christ as my Lord.	I trust Christ as my Savior and Lord.
As a result, my freedom is lost because I'm ruled by the law.	As a result, my freedom is lost because I'm ruled by selfish desires.	As a result, my freedom is truly enjoyed because the Spirit enables me to choose what is good.

Table 5.1

1. Where are you on this table?
2. What do you need to do to move to the third column?
3. Pick five words that describe your character.
4. How would you like to change?
5. What should you do next?

Voices of the Reformation: The Bondage of the Will

The Bondage of the Will was, as we've seen, Luther's response to Erasmus. We're enslaved by sin, says Luther, so that we're bound to reject God. But we don't reject God because some external force compels us against our will; what holds us in bondage are our own proud and sinful desires. Only the Holy Spirit can set us free to be the people we're meant to be.

> Salvation is beyond our own powers and devices, and depends on the work of God alone. . . .
>
> When a man is without the Spirit of God he does not do evil against his will, as if he were taken by the scruff of the neck and forced to it, like a thief or robber carried off against his will to punishment, but he does it of his own accord and with a ready will. And this readiness or will to act he cannot by his own powers omit, restrain, or change, but he keeps on willing and being ready; and even if he is compelled by external force to do something different, yet the will within him remains averse and he is resentful at whatever compels or resists it. He would not be resentful, however, if it were changed and he willingly submitted to the compulsion. . . .
>
> The will cannot change itself and turn in a different direction, but is rather the more provoked into willing by being resisted, as its resentment shows. This would not happen if it were free or had free choice. Ask experience how impossible it is to persuade people who have set their heart on anything. If they yield, they yield to force or to the greater attraction of something else; they never yield freely. On the other hand, if they are not set on anything, they simply let things take their course.
>
> By contrast, if God works in us, the will is changed, and being gently breathed upon by the Spirit of God, it again wills and acts from pure willingness and inclination and of its own accord, not from compulsion, so that it cannot be turned another way by any opposition, nor be overcome or

compelled even by the gates of hell, but it goes on willing and delighting in and loving the good, just as before it willed and delighted in and loved evil. This again is proved by experience, which shows how invincible and steadfast holy men are, who when force is used to compel them to other things are thereby all the more spurred on to will the good, just as fire is fanned into flames rather than extinguished by the wind.[11]

NOTES

Chapter 1

1. Cited in Henry Bettenson and Chris Maunder, eds., *Documents of the Christian Church*, 4th ed. (New York: Oxford University Press, 2011), 214.
2. William Tyndale, *A Pathway into the Holy Scripture*, in *The Works of William Tyndale*, ed. Henry Walter (1848–1850; repr., Carlisle, PA: Banner of Truth, 2010), 1:8, 11.
3. Tyndale, "Preface to the Five Books of Moses," in *Works*, 1:398–99.
4. Tyndale, "The Practice of Prelates," in *Works*, 2:333.
5. Cited in David Daniell, *William Tyndale: A Biography* (New Haven, CT: Yale University Press, 1994), 95.
6. Tyndale, *The Obedience of a Christian Man*, in *Works*, 1:317.
7. Huldrych Zwingli, "The Clarity and Certainty of the Word of God," in *Zwingli and Bullinger*, ed. G. W. Bromiley, Library of Christian Classics 24 (Louisville: Westminster John Knox, 1953), 68, 75, 86–87.

Chapter 2

1. Adapted from Martin Luther, *The Freedom of a Christian*, in *Selected Writings of Martin Luther*, ed. Theodore G. Tappert, vol. 2, *1520–1523* (Minneapolis: Fortress, 2007), 27.
2. For my perspective on the New Perspective, see Tim Chester, "Justification, Ecclesiology and the New Perspective," *Themelios* 30, no. 2 (2005): 5–20. Available online at http://themelios.thegospelcoalition.org/issue/30-2.
3. Martin Luther, *Second Lectures on Galatians*, cited in Gerald Bray, ed., *Galatians, Ephesians*, vol. 10 in *Reformation Commentary on Scripture: New Testament* (Downers Grove, IL: IVP Academic, 2011), 172.

4. This image is adapted from Timothy Keller, *Center Church: Doing Balanced, Gospel-Centered Ministry in Your City* (Grand Rapids, MI: Zondervan, 2012), 48.
5. Elder D. J. Ward, "Jesus Paid It All," T4G video, www.youtube.com/watch?v=JiyI35bf-io.
6. Cited in Alister E. McGrath, *Intellectuals Don't Need God and Other Modern Myths: Building Bridges to Faith through Apologetics* (Grand Rapids, MI: Zondervan, 1993), 15.
7. Augustine, *Confessions*, 1.1.
8. Luther, *Second Lectures on Galatians*, cited in Bray, *Galatians, Ephesians*, 119.
9. John Calvin, *Calvin's Commentaries*, vol. 11, *The Epistles of Paul the Apostle to the Galatians, Ephesians, Philippians, and Colossians*, trans. T. H. L. Parker, ed. David W. Torrance and Thomas F. Torrance (Edinburgh: Saint Andrew's Press, 1965), 42.
10. Martin Luther, *Galatians*, ed. Alister McGrath and J. I. Packer, Crossway Classic Commentaries (Wheaton, IL: Crossway, 1998), xx, xxi, xxii–xxiii.

Chapter 3

1. Martin Luther, *Preface to the Letter of St. Paul to the Romans (1522)*, trans. Brother Andrew Thornton, Saint Anselm Abbey, 1983, www.ccel.org/l/luther/romans/pref_romans.html.
2. Martin Luther, *Second Lectures on Galatians*, cited in Gerald Bray, ed., *Galatians, Ephesians*, vol. 10 in *Reformation Commentary on Scripture: New Testament* (Downers Grove, IL: IVP Academic, 2011), 119.
3. John Calvin, *Institutes of the Christian Religion*, ed. John T. McNeill, trans. Ford Lewis Battles, Library of Christian Classics 20–21 (Philadelphia: Westminster, 1960), 4.1.4, 9–10.

Chapter 4

1. L. P. Hartley, *The Go-Between* (Harmondsworth: Penguin, 2004), 5.
2. John Stott, *The Message of Galatians*, The Bible Speaks Today (Downers Grove, IL: InterVarsity Press, 1968), 105.
3. John Calvin, *Institutes of the Christian Religion*, ed. John T. McNeill, trans. Ford Lewis Battles, Library of Christian Classics 20–21 (Philadelphia: Westminster, 1960), 3.20.36.
4. Calvin, *Institutes*, 3.20.36–37.
5. Calvin, *Institutes*, 3.20.36–37.

Chapter 5

1. Martin Luther, *The Bondage of the Will*, in *Luther and Erasmus: Free Will and Salvation*, ed. E. Gordon Rupp and Philip S. Watson, Library of Christian Classics 17 (Philadelphia: Westminster, 1969), 333.
2. Erasmus, *The Freedom of the Will*, in Rupp and Watson, *Luther and Erasmus*, 47.
3. Luther, *Bondage of the Will*, 175.
4. Cited in Timothy George, *Theology of the Reformers* (Leicester, UK: Apollos, 1988), 72.
5. John Stott, adapting an image from William Temple, in *Basic Christianity* (Downers Grove, IL: InterVarsity Press, 2012), 102.
6. John Calvin, *Institutes of the Christian Religion*, ed. John T. McNeill, trans. Ford Lewis Battles, Library of Christian Classics 20–21 (Philadelphia: Westminster, 1960), 3.3.3, 5.
7. Martin Luther, *Martin Luther: Selections from His Writings*, ed. John Dillenberger (Garden City, NY: Anchor Books, 1961), 490.
8. For more on this theme, see Tim Chester, *You Can Change: God's Transforming Power for Our Sinful Behavior and Negative Emotions* (Wheaton, IL: Crossway, 2010).
9. Daniel Yankelovich, *New Rules: Searching for Self-Fulfillment in a World Turned Upside Down* (New York: Random House, 1981).
10. David Wells, *The Courage to Be Protestant: Truth Lovers, Marketers, and Emergents in the Postmodern World* (Grand Rapids, MI: Eerdmans, 2008), 152.
11. Luther, *Bondage of the Will*, 139–40.

GENERAL INDEX

SCRIPTURE INDEX

Made in the USA
Columbia, SC
03 April 2024